The
SUPER-SIZED BOOK

Of BIBLE PUZZLES

rainbowpublishers®
P.O. Box 261129, San Diego, CA 92196
www.RainbowPublishers.com

The
SUPER-SIZED BOOK
Of BIBLE PUZZLES

Zachary

The Super-Sized Book of Bible Puzzles
© 2013 by Rainbow Publishers
ISBN 10: 1-58411-142-9
ISBN 13: 978-1-58411-142-9
Rainbow Reorder#: RB38251
JUVENILE NONFICTION / Religious / Christian / Games & Activities

rainbowpublishers®

P.O. Box 261129
San Diego, CA 92196
www.RainbowPublishers.com

Printed in the United States of America

Table of Contents

Table of Contents

Table of Contents

Table of Contents

Table of Contents

Introduction

The SUPER-SIZED BOOK

Of BIBLE PUZZLES

Some would say we live in a puzzling world.

But others say the fun in life is solving the world's puzzles!
Why not let your kids get all the practice they need with a gigantic, huge, enormous, whopping book jammed full of puzzles. **The Super-Sized Book of Bible Puzzles** allows children to stretch their brain muscles in a fun way while they solve clever puzzles by using the Bible. Kids love to spend their time unraveling a challenging puzzle.

The Super-Sized Book of Bible Puzzles is not only a good way to keep young minds occupied, it's a great way to allow children to learn valuable Bible lessons that they can use throughout their lives.

Hours of Bible learning adventure!

This book lets kids learn about God's Word by themselves in a fun yet challenging way. A variety of exciting mind benders are provided, including word searches, crossword puzzles, mazes, word scrambles and connect-the-dot pages. Answers are provided at the back of the book.

Follow the Bible story from beginning to end, starting with the action-packed Old Testament and on through the wonderful joy of our Savior's birth to Resurrection!

Bible learning with pencils and crayons: Have a Bible on

hand. **The Super-Sized Book of Bible Puzzles** requires active use of the Bible. All the puzzles contain a brief Bible story and most pages have a memory verse. Children are encouraged to look up Scriptures to help solve the puzzles. You will also need sharpened pencils and a selection of crayons. Children can solve the puzzles by writing directly on the pages; and there are plenty of pictures that kids can color. It's a fantastic way to learn Bible lessons while having a good time!

Puzzle fun awaits! The Super-Sized Book of Bible Puzzles is a great gift for kids,

and can be used for quality family time. **The Super-Sized Book of Bible Puzzles** is sure to provide hours of big time-fun!

God Created Light

memory verse
. . . .
God said, "Let there be light, and there was light." ~Genesis 1:3

The Source of Light (Genesis 1:1-5)

God created light first because He knew how important light is. We get light from several different sources such as candles, lamps or flashlights. Do you know the source of all light? God is the source of all light.

What to Do

✳ In this picture are many different sources of light. Circle them. On the table in the picture is a Bible. The Bible tells us about God, the source of all light.

Are You My Family?

memory verse

He created them male and female ... and called them "Mankind." ~Genesis 5:2

The First Family (Genesis 1:1-31, 4:1-2 & 5:1-2)

When Adam and Eve disobeyed God, they could no longer live in the garden where it was easy to find food. Instead, they worked hard to grow their own food. They raised flocks for both food and clothing. Adam and Eve had two sons. The oldest one was named Cain. The youngest was Abel. They were the very first family in all of God's creation.

What to Do

✳ You belong to a special family because you are part of God's big family! Draw a line to the animal pairs that belong together. It's easy to pick out the animals that belong together because they look like each other.

Let's Hide Word Search

memory verse

The man and his wife heard the sound of the Lord God as he was walking in the garden in the cool of the day, and they hid from the Lord God. ~Genesis 3:8

God Sees Everything (Genesis 3)

Adam and Eve lived in a garden God made for them called the Garden of Eden. God told Adam that he and Eve could eat from any tree except the one in the middle of the garden, called the Tree of the Knowledge of Good and Evil. But a serpent, who was really Satan, told Eve if she ate from the tree she could become powerful like God. Eve ate from the tree, then she gave some to Adam to eat. Adam and Eve heard God walking by, so they tried to hide from Him because they knew they had disobeyed Him. But God sees everything we do. He already knew that they had disobeyed. As punishment, He told them they could no longer live in the beautiful garden.

What to Do

✱ Find the words from the Bible story that are hidden in the word search puzzle and circle them with different colors of pencils.

Adam   walking   tree   Eve   garden   live   disobey

ate   serpent   God   hid   longer   obey   fruit

L	N	E	D	R	A	G	T	R	E
O	W	V	O	E	T	N	D	E	V
D	A	I	B	E	E	I	T	O	A
T	U	L	O	P	S	K	U	T	G
R	I	B	R	O	N	L	O	R	N
E	T	E	B	A	D	A	M	A	F
G	S	E	V	G	I	W	T	F	R
N	Y	R	E	E	H	A	R	R	O
O	O	T	D	S	I	O	E	Y	B
L	I	V	Y	E	B	O	B	I	D

13

When Temptation Strikes

memory verse

The serpent was more crafty than any of the wild animals the LORD God had made. He said to the woman, "Did God really say, 'You must not eat from any tree in the garden?'" ~Genesis 3:1

Temptation (Genesis 3)

Why is it hard to obey when someone tells you not to do something? It's especially hard to resist doing something bad when someone makes it sound so good. That's called temptation. The serpent, which was really Satan, told Eve she would be like God if she ate from the forbidden tree. The temptation was too great for Eve and she ate fruit from the tree even though there were so many other trees in the garden bearing delicious fruit. Then Eve offered the fruit to Adam, and he ate it even though God had told him not to eat fruit from the tree. Because Adam and Eve disobeyed God, they were banned from the beautiful Garden of Eden forever.

What to Do

✳ Temptation can happen anywhere and at anytime. Look up each Scripture passage below. Then unscramble the sentence below to find how and where to get strength to resist temptation.

1. When you are tempted to lie, remember: Proverbs 19:5
2. When you are tempted to steal, remember: Leviticus 19:11
3. When you are tempted to swear, remember: Ephesians 4:29
4. When you are tempted to make fun of someone, remember: Philippians 2:3-4
5. When you are tempted to cheat, remember: Colossians 3:23
6. When you are tempted to gossip, remember: Proverbs 16:28
7. When you are tempted to smoke, drink or do drugs, remember: 1 Corinthians 10:13

Stumib	sleversuoy,	neth,	ot	dGo.
_____	_____	____	___	____

steRis	het	ledvi,	nda	eh
_____	____	_____	____	____

lilw	elef	romf	uoy.	(James 4:7)
_____	____	_____	____	

God Delivers a Baby

memory verse

Before I was born the Lord called me. ~Isaiah 49:1

Wiggly, Squiggly Babies (Genesis 4:1-2)

Adam and Eve were the first people that God created. They were husband and wife. They found out they were going to have a baby! Do you think they knew what a baby was? They had never seen one before! There were no doctors or hospitals to help deliver the new baby. But they had someone better. God helped Eve bring her son into the world. Eve said, "God helped me to give birth to a little man." She named him Cain. Soon God helped Adam and Eve give birth to another son named Abel. They were very happy. God knows who we are even before we are born!

What to Do

✱ Draw a line from each picture to its twin.

Lost in Jealousy

memory verse
. . . .
In your anger do not sin. ~Ephesians 4:26

God Likes You Best (Genesis 4:1-16)

Adam and Eve had a son named Cain, then they had another son named Abel.
One day Cain killed Abel because he was jealous of him. God punished Cain by sending him from his home and gardens. God does not want us to be jealous of others. He wants us to be happy!

What to Do

✴ Read the poem.
Your crayon is going
on a journey. Start with
Abel, then go to each
picture. You will end up
at our memory verse,
in the Bible.

Abel looked at his sheep
One, Two, Three.
He wanted his offering to God
To be the best that it could be!

Cain looked at his veggies,
Peas, beans and corn.
But God liked Abel's offering,
Oh, if his brother had not
been born!

Cain frowned at his brother,
He hated him, you see.
Then he killed brother Abel,
All because of his jealousy.

Abel

In your anger
do not sin.
Ephesians 4:26

The First Family

memory verse
God sets the lonely in families. ~Psalm 68:6

Working Together (Genesis 4:2-3)
Adam and Eve and their sons were the first family. God gives us families because He loves us. He does not want us to be lonely. Each family member has a special job.

What to Do

✴ Look at this picture. Can you tell what each person's job was? Cain was a farmer. Abel took care of the sheep. Adam fished and Eve sewed. Hidden in this picture are tools that each person needs. Can you find them? There is a spear, a shepherd's staff, a garden hoe and some thread and a needle. Draw a line to the person who will use each tool.

Noah's Sons Work Hard

memory verse
. . . .
Do what is right and good in the Lord's sight. ~Deuteronomy 6:18

Helping the Animals (Genesis 5:32; 6:8-7:1; 9:18-20)

Noah's sons, Shem, Ham and Japheth, must have worked very hard helping their father.
There was a lot of work to be done in the ark. The animals had to be fed and watered.
Food had to be prepared for the meals. The animals' pens had to be kept cleaned and
filled with fresh straw. God likes when we help each other and work hard.

What to Do

✳ Look at these
pictures. Some of
these things might
have been used
by Noah's sons.
Some of these
things we use
today. Draw a
line from the
Bible-times item
to the matching
item we use today.

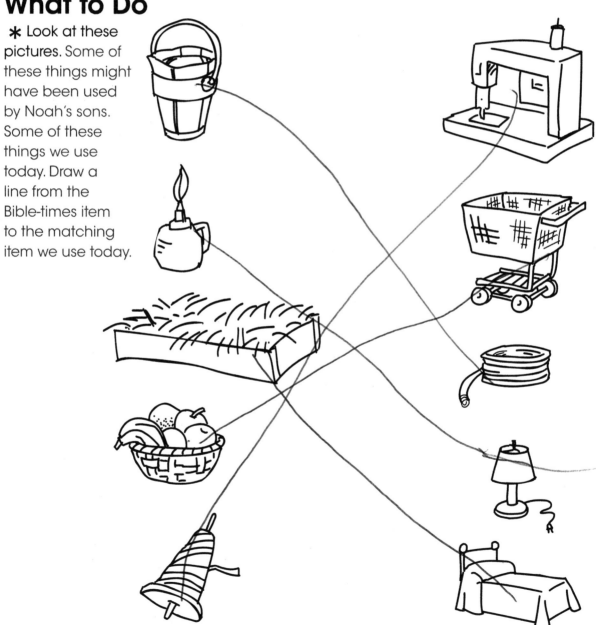

Is Dad Crazy?

memory verse
. . . .
Children, obey your parents in the Lord. ~Ephesians 6:1

Hard Work (Genesis 5:32; 6:9-7:1)

Did you know that Noah was 600 years old when he went into the ark? People lived a long time when God first made the world. When Noah was 500 years old he had three sons, Shem, Ham and Japheth. While they grew up these three boys helped their father build a big boat. Everyone laughed at Noah. Do you think the boys ever wondered if their dad was a little crazy? Probably. But they continued to obey Noah and helped him build the ark. Who do you think was laughing when it started to rain? Not Noah's sons!

What to Do

✱ Connect the dots to see what Noah and his sons built.

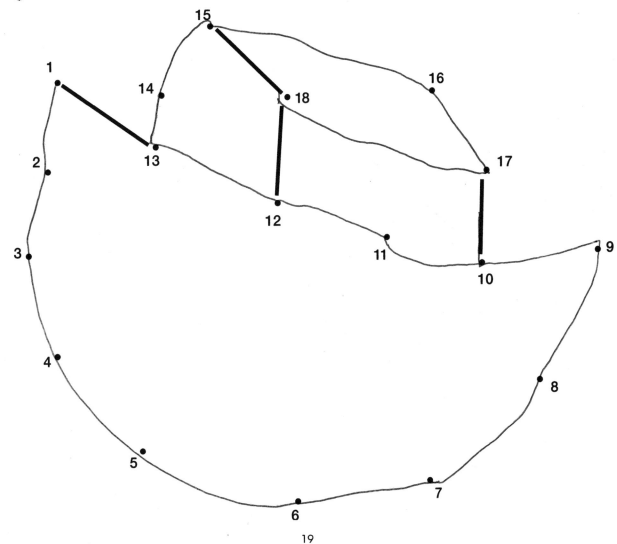

How to Float a Zoo

memory verse
....
The Lord then said to Noah, "Go into the ark, you and your whole family, because I have found you righteous in this generation." ~Genesis 7:1

Noah, His Family and the Animals
Go Into the Ark (Genesis 6:1-22 & 7:1-5)

It took Noah a long time to build the ark. When he was finished, God told him to bring on board two of each animal: a male and a female. He was also to bring seven of each bird. Noah brought all the animals and birds on the ark. Next, he stored food for everyone, including the animals. Along with his family, Noah boarded the ark. God closed the door behind them. After seven days, it began to rain. And rain, and rain!

What to Do

✱ Find and circle the words in the word search. They can be backward, horizontal, vertical or diagonal. The letters may also overlap with one another.

There is a hidden message in the leftover letters. Read from left to right, starting at the top and going down. Write each letter on the lines below until you have the complete message.

Word List

animals	flood
ark	food
birds	forty
creatures	male
days	nights
destroyed	seven
families	unclean
female	waters

```
D N D O A H D F I D E V
E E R O N A E L C N U Y
Y T N H O M I N S S G J
O S U E A F B S E Y T A
R L S L V I G I O T A D
T A E C R E L O N R M D
S M M D A I S I S O N D
E I S E M E G D R F H I
D N M A L H . Q E Q K L
M A F A T W K R T R T W
N G M S E R U T A E R C
N N J D O O L F W K T C
```

Hidden Message:

___ ____ ____ _____ ___ ____ _____ __ ___

_____ ___.

Noah Leads the Animals

memory verse

Pairs of all creatures came to Noah. ~Genesis 7:15

The Animals Obeyed God (Genesis 7:15)

God must have spoken to the animals and told them to follow Noah into the ark. The animals obeyed God and Noah, and they were all saved from the Flood.

What to Do

✳ Draw a line to each animal pair's shadow.

Animal Hunt

memory verse

The Lord then said to Noah, "Go into the ark." ~Genesis 7:1

Noah's Family (Genesis 7:1-23)

When God decided to send a flood, He told Noah to build an ark. When the ark was finished, God told Noah to bring two of every creature on the earth into the ark. One of each animal was a female and the other a male. Noah was also to bring seven of every kind of bird. Noah, his family, the animals and birds all lived on the ark.

It must have been a big job for Noah and his family to take care of all the animals and birds. God helped Noah and his family to have strength to feed and take care of the animals. He will help you with your life, too, if you just ask Him.

What to Do

✳ Look in the puzzle to find and circle animals that were on the ark that Noah built.

<u>Words to Find</u>

TIGER

ELEPHANT

SHEEP

DOVE

LION

GIRAFFE

RAVEN

G	I	D	O	T	S	E	E
I	E	N	O	I	L	L	I
R	R	A	V	V	E	S	H
A	A	F	G	P	E	L	S
F	V	E	H	E	L	E	H
F	E	A	S	H	E	P	E
E	N	S	N	A	K	E	E
T	I	R	E	G	I	T	P

Dry Land Code

memory verse
He waited seven more days and again sent out the dove. ~Genesis 8:10

Noah Sends out the Dove (Genesis 7:17-24 & 8:1-12)

When it began to rain, it didn't stop for 40 days and nights! Water covered the earth. Noah's family had a long wait for dry land. After months of watching the water go down, Noah sent a raven to find dry land. It flew back, so Noah knew the land was not yet dry. He waited longer, then sent out a dove to check for dry land again. The first time it didn't find dry land. The second time, it brought back an olive leaf, so Noah knew the land was beginning to dry. The third time, it didn't come back at all. Noah knew the land must be dry.

What to Do

✱ Solve the secret message below by substituting the letters for the numbers listed. You will then need to unscramble the letters within each word to get the correct word.

A-26 J-13 S-25
B-3   K-9   T-4
C-1   L-24 U-16
D-2   M-15 V-12
E-8   N-18 W-29
F-14 O-10 X-23
G-11 P-21 Y-22
H-6   Q-31 Z-35
I-7   R-20

How did God tell Noah that it was time to leave the ark?

E T H   V O E D   F U N O D   Y D R   O L A N.
8 4 6   12 10 8 2   14 16 18 10 2   22 2 20   2 24 26 18

The _____

_____

The Long Voyage

memory verse
. . . .
In its beak was a freshly plucked olive leaf!   ~Genesis 8:11

The Dove Returns (Genesis 8:6-12)

Have you ever gone on a long trip? Noah and his family were on a long, tiring ride through a flood. After 40 days and 40 nights of rain, the skies cleared. Noah opened a window and sent a raven to search for dry land, but it did not find any. Then Noah sent a dove. On its second flight it returned with an olive leaf in its mouth. Noah knew the dove must have taken the leaf from an olive tree on dry land somewhere. Soon their long trip would be over. Noah and his family must have been very tired from riding on the ark. God protected them from the flood, just as He said He would. God will protect you, too.

What to Do

✶ Match the number of the word with the number of the blank. Write the correct word in each blank.

It rained for __forty__ __days__ and __forty__ __nights__.
                 1   9   1   4

__Noah__ first __sent__ out a __raven__ and then a __dove__
   2   10   7   6

to find dry __land__. The dove found an olive __leaf__.
           8   5

1. ~~forty~~
2. ~~Noah~~
3. animals
4. ~~nights~~
5. leaf

6. ~~dove~~
7. ~~raven~~
8. ~~land~~
9. ~~days~~
10. ~~sent~~

The Dove Returns to the Ark

memory verse
. . . .
The dove returned to him. ~Genesis 8:11

Noah Releases a Dove (Genesis 8:6-12)

Noah and his family went in the ark with all the animals during the flood. He released a dove to see if it would locate land. What could Noah have been thinking while waiting for the dove to return? Noah obeyed God and stayed in the ark until God said it was time to come out. We should obey God, too, and live as He says.

What to Do

✳ Follow the maze with your finger or a pencil.

25

Mystery Word

memory verse

I have set my rainbow in the clouds. ~Genesis 9:13

God Gives Noah a Promise (Genesis 8:13-9:17)

Noah, his family and all the animals were on the ark for many months. When the land was dry, God told Noah and the others to leave the ark. The first thing Noah did when he got off the ark was build an altar to praise God. As Noah worshipped, God promised him He would never flood the earth again. As a sign of His promise to Noah, God put a rainbow in the sky each time it rained. Whenever you see a rainbow, be reminded that God always keeps His promise.

What to Do

✱ You will be looking for a mystery word. Fill in the blanks of the numbered phrases, then write the first letter of each word on the Mystery Word line. Then color the rainbow.

1. Noah was on the ark because it was _r_aining.

2. God told Noah to build an _a_rk.

3. The rainbow was _i_n the sky.

4. God made a promise to _n_oah.

Mystery Word:

r a i n b o w

5. Noah _b_uilt an altar to thank God.

6. God gave Noah a sign _o_f His promise.

7. God _w_as pleased with the altar.

The Big Tower

memory verse
....
Pride goes before destruction, a haughty spirit before a fall. ~Proverbs 16:18

God Stops a Big Tower (Genesis 11:1-9)

Some people built a big tower. They wanted to reach heaven because they thought they were more important than God. These people were very prideful. God does not like pride. He stopped the people from making the big tower. He made them speak in different languages so they could not talk to each other. This made it very hard to continue working on the big tower. The people had to leave the big tower and make new homes in other places. They were not so proud anymore. They knew that they needed God. We need God, too.

What to Do

✳ Follow the maze to find your way to the top of the BIG tower and back down again.

Start

Finish

Abraham Moves to Canaan

memory verse
. . . .
By faith Abraham obeyed and went. ~Hebrews 11:8

A Big Move (Genesis 12)

Have you ever moved to a new home? How did you feel? Abraham left his home and traveled far away. God told him where to go. Abraham obeyed God.

What to Do

✴ Cross out the lower-case letters. The letters that remain tell where Abraham went. Then color the picture.

w C r t A q N p z A g i A k N

Blessings Maze

memory verse
. . . .
The Lord had said to Abram, "Leave your country." ~Genesis 12:1

God Tells Abram to Leave His Country (Genesis 12:1-9)

Abram was 75 years old when God told him to leave his land and go to another country. He took Sarai, his wife, and Lot, his nephew, with him. They packed up all their possessions and set out for Canaan. It must have been difficult to leave family and friends behind. Abram loved, worshipped and trusted God. Because Abram obeyed God, He promised to bless Abram's family.

You can please God and obey your parents and teachers. How do you feel when you disobey them? How do you feel when you obey them?

What to Do

✷ Follow the path Abram took to the new land.

CANAAN

A Special Son

memory verse

Abram believed the Lord ~Genesis 15:6

Babies Need Lots of Things (Genesis 15:1; 21:1-7)

God promised Abraham many children and grandchildren. But Sarah, his wife, was very old. She thought it was too late to have a baby. Yet Abraham believed God. They did have a very special son. They named him Isaac, which means laughter. Isaac made Abraham and Sarah very happy.

What to Do

✳ In each row, circle the item that was not used in Bible times.

A Faithful Father

memory verse

Now faith is being sure of what we hope for and certain of what we do not see.

~Hebrews 11:1

Faith in the Unseen (Genesis 15:1-6; 17:1-22)

God promised Abraham that his descendants would be as numerous as the stars. Abraham believed God would keep His promise. For many years Abraham had no children. How could God keep His promise without children being born to Abraham? Finally, when Abraham and his wife Sarah were really old, they had a son. Abraham trusted and had faith in God, even though it looked like it would never happen. Do you believe God will keep His promises?

What to Do

* Color all the shapes with a dot to see what Abraham had.

God Cares for Abraham's Son

memory verse
....
The Lord their God will care for them. ~Zephaniah 2:7

An Angel Arrives (Genesis 16:1-13; 21:1-20)

Abraham was the father of Ishmael and Isaac. Sarah, Abraham's wife, was jealous of Hagar and her son, Ishmael, who made fun of Isaac. So she sent them back to Egypt where Hagar's family lived. Abraham was sad, but God promised to take care of Ishmael. On the way, Hagar and Ishmael got lost, tired and thirsty. Hagar didn't want to watch her son die. She put him under a bush for shade and went away and cried. Just then she heard a voice: "Don't be afraid. God will take care of you and the boy." Hagar looked up and saw an angel standing before her. Then she saw water flowing out of rocks nearby. God cared for Ishmael. He will care for you, too.

What to Do

✱ What did Hagar lay Ishmael under? Finish drawing it. Who talked to Hagar? Connect the dots to find out. What came out of the rocks? Draw it.

Sarah Has a Son

memory verse

The Lord has brought me laughter. ~Genesis 21:6

Messengers Deliver
Good News (Genesis 18:10-15; 21:1-7)

Sarah wanted children very much. But Sarah never had children when she was young. Then, when she was very old, three visitors came to see her and her husband, Abraham. They were messengers from God. The Lord wanted Abraham to know that He would keep His promise to give him and Sarah a son. When Sarah heard this, she laughed, "After I am old and tired, will I now have a son?" The messenger scolded Sarah, "Is anything too hard for the Lord?" Do you think Sarah had a son? Yes, she did! She named him "Isaac," which means "laughter." Sarah laughed because she was so happy to have a child.

What to Do

* There are eight things that don't belong in this picture. Circle the things that Sarah would not have had for Isaac in Bible times.

Isaac is Born

memory verse
. . . .
And so after waiting patiently, Abraham received what was promised.

~Hebrews 6:15

A Special Son (Genesis 21:1-7)

God loved Abraham very much. Abraham was a good man who loved God. God made a very special promise to Abraham. God promised Abraham a son. But the years went by and Abraham and Sarah had no son. Abraham was 100 years old. Sarah was too old to have a baby. But God kept His promise. He gave Abraham and Sarah a son. They named their baby "Isaac," which means "laughter." Do you think they laughed with happiness over their new son? God keeps His promises.

What to Do

✱ There are a lot of silly things in this picture that don't belong in biblical times. Circle the things that don't make sense.

34

Find the Sheep

memory verse

We must obey God. ~Acts 5:29

A True Test **of Love** (Genesis 22:1-18)

God decided to test Abraham to see if Abraham loved his son Isaac more than Abraham loved God. God told Abraham to bring Isaac to a mountain and sacrifice (or kill) the boy. Abraham obeyed God by bringing Isaac to the mountain. Just when he was ready to sacrifice his son, an angel told Abraham, "Stop." Abraham sacrificed a sheep instead. This story shows us that Abraham loved God most of all.

What to Do

✳ Help Abraham find the sheep in the bushes. Glue a piece of cotton on the sheep when you find it. What other animals do you see? Color the picture. As you color, think of ways you can show God you love Him. Say, "Thank You, God, for giving me the Bible so that I can learn how to love You more."

A Young Girl Shows Kindness

memory verse
....
I will follow you wherever you go. ~Luke 9:57

Rebekah at the Well (Genesis 24)

Isaac grew up in the land of Canaan. Abraham did not want Isaac to marry an idol worshiper from Canaan, so he sent a servant to find a wife for Isaac. The servant prayed that God would show him the right girl. As he sat by the city well he prayed, "Have her offer me and my camel a drink of water." Just then a beautiful girl, Rebekah, walked up and did just that. Rebekah returned to Canaan with the servant and married Isaac.

What to Do

✱ Rebekah gathered water at the well. Draw a line between the jars that are alike.

Twin Brothers

memory verse

Jacob I loved. ~Romans 9:13

Two Sons (Genesis 25:19-28)

Isaac and Rebekah wanted a child. They prayed, "God, please give us a baby." Do you think God answered their prayer? He did! He gave them twins, Esau and Jacob. Esau was a great hunter. But God had a special plan for Jacob. His family would become God's special people, the Israelites. God would do special things for Jacob's family.

What to Do

✳ How many things in the top picture are different from the one below?

Very Different Twins

memory verse

. . . .

We have different gifts. ~Romans 12:6

Different Boys (Genesis 25:19-27)

Esau and Jacob were twins but they were very different boys. Esau loved to hunt and be outdoors. Jacob was more quiet and stayed near home. Isaac, their father, favored Esau because he loved wild game. Rebekah, their mother, enjoyed Jacob, who helped her cook and work among the tents. Each of us is very special.

What to Do

✱ Draw a line between Esau and the things he might have liked. Then draw a line between Jacob and what he might have used.

ESAU   JACOB

Happy are the Peacemakers

memory verse
Blessed are the peacemakers, for they will be called sons of God. ~Matthew 5:9

Finding Peace (Genesis 26:12-33)

God loved Isaac. Isaac loved and obeyed God. Isaac lived near the Philistines who did not love God. They worshipped idols. God blessed Isaac and gave him good things. The Philistines grew jealous. They did not want Isaac to be happy. One day the Philistines filled Isaac's well with dirt. Isaac had no water. Do you think Isaac got mad? No, he just moved and dug another well. But the Philistines stole that well, too. Again, Isaac didn't fight, he just moved. Three times Isaac moved instead of fighting. Finally Isaac built a well that the Philistines did not want. Isaac was happy. God was happy that Isaac was a peacemaker. God is happy when we are peacemakers and choose not to fight.

What to Do

* Isaac refused to fight the Philistines. Follow this maze to help Isaac finally find a peaceful place.

WHO? Worksheet

A Sneaky Twin (Genesis 27:1-20)

Esau and Jacob were twins. Esau was the oldest twin, so he would inherit their father's special blessing. Esau was his father, Isaac's, favorite son. He liked to hunt. Jacob was his mother, Rebekah's, favorite. He liked to stay near home.

Jacob knew that Esau would get their father's blessing. Jacob wished that he had been born first. "Why can't Father give me the blessing?" he would ask with a jealous heart.

What to Do

* Read the story above and the questions below. Use the correct colors to answer the questions.

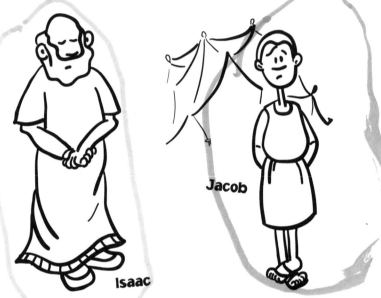

1. Who was the daddy of Jacob and Esau?
Draw a circle around him with a green crayon.

2. Who was the mommy of Jacob and Esau?
Draw a circle around her with a blue crayon.

3. Who was the brother who liked to hunt?
Draw a circle around him with a red crayon.

4. Who was the brother who liked to stay at home?
Draw a circle around him with a purple crayon.

40

Honest Before God

memory verse
. . . .
He said, "Your brother came deceitfully and took your blessing." ~Genesis 27:35

Jacob Deceives His Father (Genesis 27:1-35)

Jacob and Esau were twin brothers. Rebekah, their mother, overheard Isaac, their old and blind father, tell Esau to prepare a special meal for him so he could give him the birthright. But Rebekah wanted Jacob to get the birthright, so she told Jacob to dress like Esau and put goatskins on his arms and neck so he could fool Isaac into thinking he was really Esau. The plan worked. Jacob received the blessing. Esau was so mad he wanted to kill his brother. Jacob ran away. God does not like it when we are deceitful like Jacob was.

What to Do

✱ Read and circle the answer for each question. Each answer has a corresponding letter. Circle the letter for the best answer, then color that letter in the grid below. When finished, look at the grid and write the letters that are NOT colored. Then unscramble the letters to make a word.

1. What would you do if you found money on the playground at school?
   A. Keep it. (I)
   B. Tell a teacher. (A)
   C. Ask your friends. (E)

2. What would you do if your friends were watching a movie you know your parents wouldn't want you to see?
   A. Watch it anyway because they will never know. (C)
   B. Watch it and ask your friends not to tell. (D)
   C. Say you don't want to watch it and leave. (O)

3. What would you do if you were shopping with your friends and the cashier gave you back too much money?
   A. Keep it because they probably overcharged you another time. (E)
   B. Tell the cashier. (H)

4. What would you do if you overheard your older brother tell another friend that he is skipping school tomorrow?
   A. Tell your parents and ask them not to tell your brother you told them. (T)
   B. Tell your brother you know about his plans and encourage him to talk to
      your parents on his own. (V)

T	V	O	D	E	H	C	E	I	A

___ ___ ___ ___ ___

A Father of Many Sons

 memory verse
....

Children are a heritage from the Lord, offspring are a reward from him.

~Psalm 127:3

God Keeps His Promise (Genesis 29:14–30:24; 35:23-26)

God promised Abraham that his descendants would be as numerous as the stars. But it wasn't until his grandchildren that the promise would be kept. His grandson, Jacob, had to leave his home and go far away because Jacob's brother Esau was angry with him. So Jacob traveled far from home. But that turned out to be a good thing because Jacob married there and had many children. Jacob had 12 sons! The promise that Abraham would have many descendants would be fulfilled. Through these sons Israel would become a great nation. We should trust God to always do good for us.

What to Do

✱ Jacob had many children, but he had 12 sons. Can you find the boys in this picture? Circle Jacob's 12 sons.

Tricked into Marriage

memory verse

Laban had two daughters. ~Genesis 29:16

Jacob Marries (Genesis 29:1-35)

After he left home, Jacob lived and worked with his Uncle Laban. Jacob wanted to marry Laban's youngest daughter, Rachel. He agreed to work for his uncle for seven years to earn the right to marry her. When the time came to marry Rachel, Laban tricked Jacob into instead marrying Leah, his oldest daughter, because the custom was for the oldest daughter to marry first. Jacob was mad, but he agreed to work another seven years so he could also marry Rachel. Laban had tricked Jacob just like Jacob had tricked his brother, but Jacob followed God and did what was right to marry Rachel anyway.

Jacob must have missed his family back home but God watched over him and gave him a new family.

What to Do

✱ Each number below is matched with a letter. Use the code to figure out the names of Jacob's two wives.

1	2	3	4	5	6	7	8	9	10	11
L	Z	H	Q	E	T	C	A	M	R	F

R A C H E L
10 8 7 3 5 1

and L E A H
1 5 8 3

Stained Glass Forgiveness

memory verse

Esau ran to meet Jacob and embraced him. ~Genesis 33:4

Jacob Returns Home (Genesis 31, 32 & 33)

Jacob lived many years in Haran with his Uncle Laban. Jacob was married. He had many children, servants and flocks. One day, God said it was time for Jacob to return to his homeland. So Jacob packed up his possessions and his family, then began the long trip home. Jacob was still afraid of his brother, Esau, whom he had tricked, so he sent servants ahead to tell Esau he was coming home. Esau ran to greet Jacob with kisses and hugs. Esau had forgiven Jacob!

Think about a time when someone was mean to you. How did you feel? Did you forgive the person? You can forgive others like Esau forgave his brother, Jacob. God wants us to be forgiving to others, just like He forgives us.

What to Do

✳ Color each part of the stained glass window according to the chart. Arrange the letters to spell what Esau did for Jacob and write it on the lines below.

F = red
O = green
R = yellow

G = purple
I = blue

V = orange
E = pink

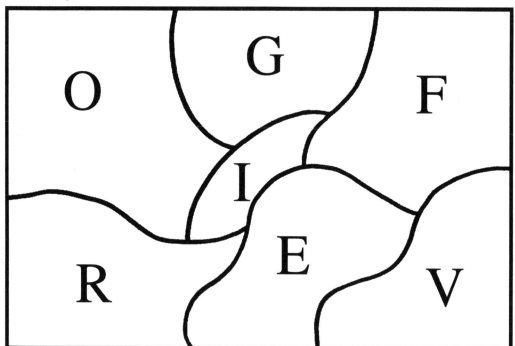

__ __ __ __ __ __ __

An Obedient Son

memory verse

Children, obey your parents. ~Ephesians 6:1

A Special Gift (Genesis 37:1-4)

Jacob had twelve sons. Joseph was Jacob's favorite son. Joseph worked hard for his father. He tended the sheep and took food to his older brothers working in the fields. Joseph was a good boy and obeyed his father, so his father gave him a special coat. If you obey God, His special gift to you will be to live with Him forever in heaven.

What to Do

✳ Which is not complete? One picture in each of the rows is only half-finished. Find those that are not complete and fill in the missing parts so they match the others.

Joseph Trusts God

memory verse
....
Trust in the Lord. ~Proverbs 3:5

God Cares for Joseph (Genesis 37:5-36)

Joseph loved God. Joseph was a good boy and his father loved him very much. But Joseph's brothers did not like him. One day they sold him into slavery. Joseph trusted God to take care of him, even in bad times. We can always trust God to take care of us.

What to Do

✳ Color the picture. Connect the dots in each letter to read the word.

His Only Possession Puzzle

memory verse

He made a richly ornamented robe for him. ~Genesis 37:3

Joseph is Sold into Captivity (Genesis 37:1-36)

Joseph had 11 brothers. The brothers had to take care of the family's sheep. Joseph was 17 when his father, Jacob, made him a beautiful robe to wear. His brothers became jealous. They stole his robe and sold Joseph to some travelers who took him to Egypt. While in Egypt, Joseph was sold as a slave. Joseph was young and far from home. His brothers had been very cruel to him, yet Joseph still believed and trusted God.

What to Do

✳ Unscramble the words below and put them in order to find what possession Joseph had with him. No one could buy, sell or take away that possession from Joseph. You can also have this possession.

D G O   T F A I H   N I   S I H

G O D   f a i t H   __ __   __ __ __

In the correct order:

h i s   f a i t H   i N   G O D

Circle the Picture

The Patient Brother (Genesis 37-50)

Joseph lived with his father, Jacob, in Canaan. Joseph had ten older brothers and one younger brother. Because Jacob loved Joseph, he made him a colorful coat. Instead of being happy that Joseph had a beautiful new coat, his brothers became angry and jealous. "When will my brothers show kindness to me?" he wondered. But Joseph was patient with his brothers. He knew God was in charge.

What to Do

* Joseph didn't have to wait on the playground, but you might have to wait your turn to go down the slide. Joseph didn't have to wait for the drinking fountain, but you might have to. You can learn to be patient — just like Joseph!

Circle the pictures of the places where Joseph had to wait. Color the picture of Joseph and his colorful coat.

A Story to Tell

memory verse

The Lord was with Joseph. ~Genesis 39:23

God Helps Joseph (Genesis 39-41)

Joseph's brothers hated him so much they sold him as a slave. One day, Joseph's master became angry with him and threw him into prison. While Joseph was in prison, the king of Egypt had two dreams. Joseph told the king what the dreams meant. The king was pleased. He made Joseph an important man. Joseph was reunited with his family. God helped Joseph to turn a bad time into a good one.

What to Do

* These pictures of Joseph are all mixed up. Can you number them in the correct order? The first one is done for you.

Forgiveness Word Search

memory verse

Joseph said to his brothers, "I am Joseph! Is my father still living?" ~Genesis 45:3

Joseph Meets his Brothers Again (Genesis 42-45)

Joseph had been a slave in Egypt for over 13 years. Now he was in charge of all the people. When the famine began, people from other countries heard that Egypt still had food. Joseph's brothers traveled from Canaan to Egypt to find food. When they met Joseph, they didn't recognize him as their brother, but Joseph knew them. He gave them food but didn't reveal who he was. When they returned, he told them who he was and forgave them.

What to Do

✱ Why is it hard to keep your faith and trust in God when the going gets rough? The words in the word key below are printed in the correct order for you to understand why God allowed Joseph to be sold into slavery 13 years earlier. Sometimes we don't understand why God allows things to happen. You can trust and have faith in God like Joseph did.

Circle each of the words in the word search below. The words can be vertical, horizontal, diagonal or backward.

Words to Find

You	intended
to	harm
me	but
God	intended
it	for
good	~~to~~
accomplish	what
~~is~~	now
being	done
the	saving
of	many
lives	

```
            A N E Z T G C L
          A N C A O R W W D E
          E B S C Q A T S T W
      D I I O E O R T U I F N
      K F E Z Z B M B A L T O
    I B T W W N O D P E J W E R
    L J D N I S R T T L O W E J
  W G D M O D S Y A V V I M H I A
Q C S E U O S S W D O V X S Y A H N
V V H R N A F U N B S O Y A H S T R
E E M W E N C G T H U I M S G E R I D
C E J O L D P A K H O T O I A R O B G S
A P J M K X W F N H B T P J B N R D N S
I Q I G H N C N D E W E E N D G Y L N T
G U L R Q R M U I U B R H B O E T H T E
S H E M O R S N I A C R N O E P R D W S
K H E H B R G G T S G A D R A V X S Y U
T X B O L T N O A F R T C E M E A W T D
O M E T X M G V I T O U L N B T G W G H
S T S L B I I A R E E R C E P D R W N R
  L G L Z N T E E S E E N G I U E A K
  N A E G M E M S F U S V Q F X I R D
    H Y D C E R T E O H D T A L N E
    L E E S L P N Z G W O Y E D
    W F H D H I N O X U O K N L
      N H I N A V I W U E E E
      Y O R N E R E R S T E B
      R L D T M S N D B
      S N E K B N I C D H
        A T G N M I A C
```

A Princess Rescues a Baby

memory verse

I trust in God's unfailing love. ~Psalm 52:8

Hidden in the Reeds (Exodus 2:1-10)

Pharaoh, the king of Egypt, did not like the Israelites living in his country. He ordered all of the Hebrew baby boys put to death. One mother did not obey. Moses' mother placed her son in a basket and floated it in the Nile River to hide him. When the Pharaoh's daughter went to the river to bathe, she found the baby and loved him. She took him home as her own son. God had special plans for this baby boy.

What to Do

✱ Follow the path to help the Egyptian princess find baby Moses in the reeds.

Helping the **Family**

memory verse
. . . .
The Lord is my helper. ~Hebrews 13:6

Miriam Watches Over Moses (Exodus 2:5-10)

Taking care of her baby brother, Moses, was a big responsibility for Miriam. She must have been very scared watching over him day after day. But she wanted to help her family and little brother. She knew that the Lord would help her. He helps all of us do what we might not be able to do on our own.

What to Do

* Circle some ways you can help your family.

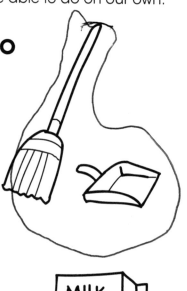

Who Sees Me Puzzle

memory verse

Then Moses was afraid. ~Exodus 2:14

Moses Flees Egypt (Genesis 4:1-2)

Moses was one of God's people who lived in Egypt. When he was a baby, his mother put him in a basket on the Nile River. Pharaoh's daughter found him and raised him as her own son. When Moses was a young man, he saw an Egyptian man hitting one of God's people. Moses thought no one was looking, so he killed the Egyptian. Someone did see him. When Pharaoh found out, he wanted to kill Moses, so Moses ran away.

God sees everything you do. He loves you and forgives you even when you do bad things. God loves you and always forgives.

What to Do

✳ Use crayons to color each part of the puzzle with the correct color as indicated on the color chart below left. When finished, there will be three places you didn't color. What word do those letters spell? Write it on the line below.

R = RED

B = BLUE

Y = YELLOW

P = PINK

_____ _____ _____

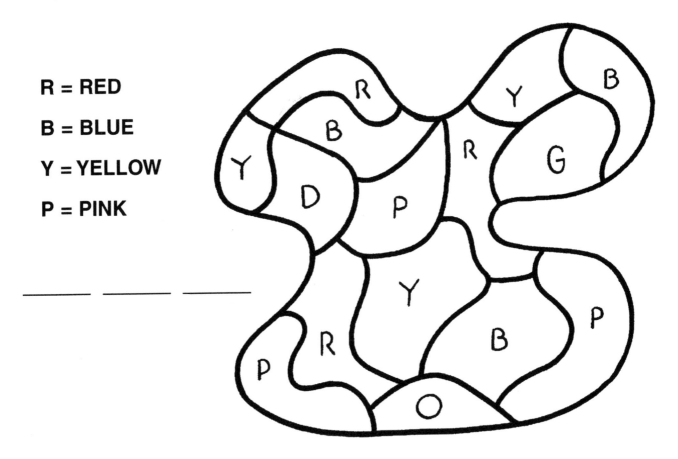

Moses Stands Up to Pharaoh

memory verse
....
No harm [comes] to the righteous. ~Proverbs 12:21

Moses is a Brave Man (Exodus 3:1-4:17; 12:37-13:16)

The king, or pharaoh, of Egypt was a bad man. He made God's people work hard as slaves and did not pay them. God told Moses to lead His people out of Egypt. Moses went to Pharaoh and demanded that he free God's people. Pharaoh said, "No! I will not let them go!" So God made bad things happen. Time and time again Moses went to Pharaoh and said, "Let God's people go!" Pharaoh was stubborn and refused to free the people. Ten bad things happened, until finally the worst thing of all happened. God caused all of the oldest boys to die. Even Pharaoh's son died. But Moses' people were kept safe because they obeyed God. So Pharaoh told Moses he could take his people and leave Egypt. Do you think Moses was brave to go before Pharaoh so many times?

What to Do

✳ Look at these pictures. They tell the story of Moses and Pharaoh. Can you number them in the order that they happened?

Plague Word Search

memory verse

Then the Lord said to Moses, "Go to Pharaoh and say to him, 'This is what the Lord says: Let my people go, so that they may worship me.'" ~Exodus 8:1

God Sends the Plagues (Exodus 4:14-16 & 6:1-12:29)

God instructed Moses and Aaron to tell Pharaoh to let God's people go to worship Him. Moses performed miraculous signs to convince Pharaoh to let the Israelites go, but each time he still refused. So God began a series of plagues on Pharaoh and the Egyptians. First, God turned the Nile River into blood. Then He sent plagues of frogs, gnats, flies, hail, locusts and darkness. Finally, God sent a plague of death on the firstborn of each household. God told the Israelites how to protect themselves against this last plague. Finally, Pharaoh was worn down. He agreed to let God's people go.

What to Do

✻ Find the words from the story in the word search. Words may be found vertically, horizontally, diagonally and backward.

Words to Find

AARON	MOSES
GNATS	FIRSTBORN
HAIL	NILE
BLOOD	FLIES
LIVESTOCK	PHARAOH
DEAD	FROGS
LOCUSTS	PLAGUE
EGYPT	RIVER

```
E K Z N J H Z C H K F
L C H O A R A H P I W
I O V I Q D A L R M N
N T L K T A O S R R P
E S G O R F T O R H S
U E T O S B S R L Z E
G V N P O E I T P B I
A I G R Y V S T A R L
L L N R E G C O N N F
P Q Q R D A E D M M G
L Y W R S T S U C O L
```

Ten Warnings

memory verse
. . . .
All rulers will worship and obey him. ~Daniel 7:27

God Warned Pharaoh (Exodus 7-11)

Moses told the king of Egypt, "Let my people go!" The king was angry and said, "No! They will stay my slaves!" Then God sent ten warnings to the king. Bad things began to happen. The king kept telling Moses, "No!" So God sent His last warning. The king's oldest son died. Now the king of Egypt knew that God was real. He let Moses and the people leave. God doesn't like it when we disobey Him, but He takes care of those who do obey Him.

What to Do

✳ How many of each creature is in this picture?
Count the creatures, then color the picture.

3 ___

6 ___

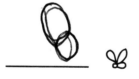

___

Moses Crosses the Red Sea

memory verse

The people put their trust in him. ~Exodus 14:31

Crossing the Red Sea (Exodus 12:31; 13-15)

The king of Egypt chased Moses and his people. When the people saw a huge sea (called the Red Sea) in front of them they got scared. But Moses told the people not to be afraid. "God will help us!" he said. And God did! He parted the sea! The people crossed onto dry land, then God closed the sea so the soldiers could not cross. God took care of Moses and His people, and He takes care of us.

What to Do

✳ Help Moses lead the Israelites across the Red Sea. Follow the path with a pencil or crayon.

Heading for the Promised Land

memory verse

I am the Lord your God, who brought you out of Egypt. ~Deuteronomy 5:6

God Guides Moses (Exodus 13:17-22)

Pharaoh finally allowed the Israelites to leave Egypt. Moses led them to the Promised Land with God's help. God sent a big cloud in the sky. Each day God's cloud showed Moses where to go. At night the cloud was gone. But God sent a big fire in the sky so Moses could see where to go at night. The boys and girls who followed Moses saw the cloud and fire, too. They knew God was helping Moses.

What to Do

✳ Connect the dots to see what led God's people in the day.

✳ Use an orange crayon to draw what led the people at night.

Match the Facts

memory verse
Moses answered the people, "Do not be afraid. Stand firm and you will see the deliverance the Lord will bring you today." ~Exodus 14:13

God Parts the Red Sea (Exodus 13:17-14:31)

God used Moses to convince Pharaoh to let God's people go. They walked until they came to the Red Sea. It was too big to cross! When they looked back, they saw the Egyptian army coming after them. Pharaoh had changed his mind! The Israelites were afraid. God told Moses to raise his staff and stretch his arm over the water. When he did, it suddenly parted. All the Israelites crossed the sea safely, but when Pharaoh's army tried, the waters closed. They all drowned. God performed a miracle when He parted the Red Sea to save the Israelites from the Egyptian army.

What to Do

✳ Do you know the answers to the questions in column A? Write the letter of the correct answer next to each question.

Column A

1. Who was the king of Egypt? ____

2. What was the name of Moses' brother? ____

3. Why was the army chasing the Israelites? ____

4. What is the name of the sea they crossed? ____

5. Of what were the Israelites afraid? ____

6. How did the Israelites cross the sea? ____

7. What did God tell Moses to do? ____

8. What happened to Pharaoh's army? ____

Column B

A. They walked across the parted sea.

B. They all drowned.

C. Pharaoh

D. Pharaoh's army

E. Aaron

F. Pharaoh had changed his mind.

G. Red Sea

H. Raise his staff and stretch out his arm.

Crossing the Red Sea

memory verse

[He] swept Pharaoh and his army into the sea. ~Psalm 136:15

Pharaoh's Chariots (Exodus 13:17-22; 14)

Pharaoh let Moses' people leave Egypt. But Pharaoh changed his mind when he realized there would be no one to do the work. So he gathered all of his soldiers to chase Moses and the people. When the people came to a large sea, they were scared. God knew what to do. He sent a big wind to blow the sea apart and the people crossed through the parted water. When Pharaoh's chariots got to the sea, God brought the water back. The sea swallowed Pharaoh's men and the chariots. Do you think that the little boys and girls with Moses ever forgot that exciting day?

What to Do

✳ Can you find the chariot that is different from the others? Circle it. Then color the picture so that all of the chariots are diferent!

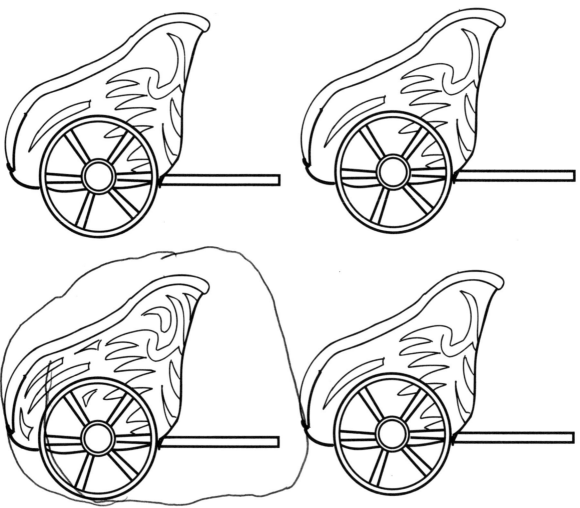

Ten Rules to Obey

memory verse

I will obey your word. ~Psalm 119:17

God's Rules (Exodus 20)

God had some very special rules He wanted the people to obey. God told Moses to go high on a mountain. There, God wrote ten rules on stone called the Ten Commandments. He gave the stones to Moses. Moses told the people the rules. Some of the people obeyed the rules. Do you want to obey God's rules? Obeying God's rules makes us happy.

What to Do

✶ Connect the dots to see where God wrote His rules.

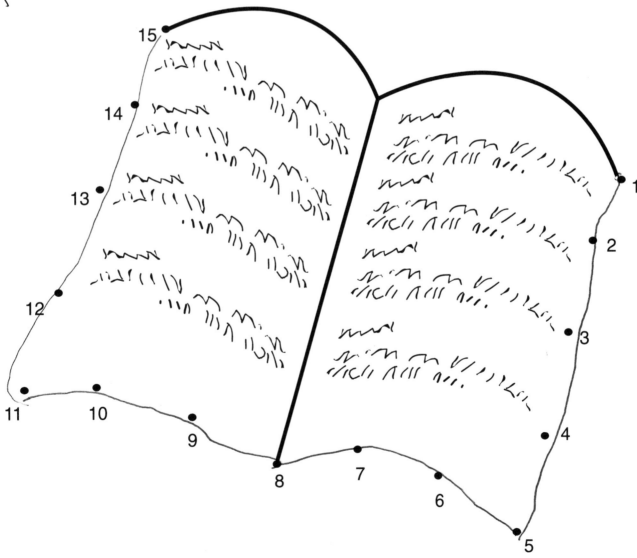

Rules About God

memory verse

As for God, his way is perfect; the word of the Lord is flawless.
He is a shield for all who take refuge in him. ~2 Samuel 22:31

One God (Exodus 20:1-11; 32:1-35)

The first four rules that God told Moses on the mountain were about God. God wanted His people to worship Him and only Him. They were not to have any other gods and were not to build idols of stone or gold. God said that His people should not use God's name in anger. They were to make sure they kept the Sabbath holy and worshipped God. When Moses came down from the mountain, he was surprised to see that some of the people had built a golden statue! They were worshipping a golden calf instead of God. They were disobeying God's first important rule. Moses was very unhappy. God was very unhappy. God punished the people who disobeyed. Because of this story we know that God is the one to worship.

What to Do

✳ The children below want to keep the Sabbath holy by going to church. Can you help them find their way?

Ten Commandments

God Sends His Laws (Exodus 20:2-4, 7-8, 12-17)

"I am the Lord your God, . . . You shall have no other gods before me. You shall not make for yourself an idol. You shall not misuse the name of the Lord your God, . . . Remember the Sabbath day by keeping it holy. Honor your father and your mother . . . You shall not murder. You shall not commit adultery. You shall not steal. You shall not give false testimony against your neighbor. You shall not covet . . . anything that belongs to your neighbor."

What to Do

✳ We all have rules that govern our lives. These rules were made by your parents, school boards, government and others. The most important set of rules was given by God to Moses many years ago. These rules are called "The Ten Commandments." Read this scripture telling about these commandments to find clues to fill in the crossword puzzle.

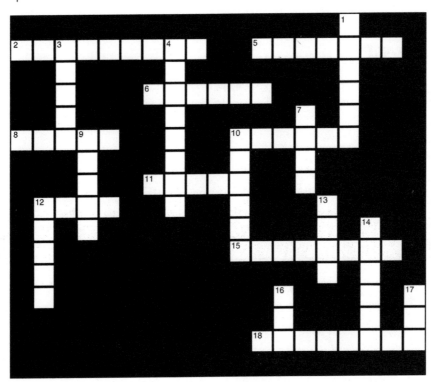

Down

1. Male parent
3. To take without permission
4. One who lives near another
7. False god
9. Formal future tense
10. Female parent
12. Esteem, respect
13. What you are called
14. Previously
16. Great Creator
17. After dawn

Across

2. Declaration of fact or truth
5. Weekly day of rest
6. To use wrongly
8. Not true
10. To kill
11. Desire that which is another's
12. Sacred
15. Not forget
18. Failure of loyalty in marriage

The Golden Calf

memory verse

. . . .

You shall have no other gods before me. ~Exodus 20:3

Worship Only God (Genesis 32)

Moses led the Israelites through a big desert. God had promised to take His people to a special land. One day Moses went up on a high mountain. God wanted to talk to Moses. Moses was gone a long time. The people said, "Moses is never coming back. Who will help us?" So the people made a statue. It was a golden calf. "The golden calf will help us. It is our new god!" the people shouted. Do you think Moses was happy when he came down from the mountain? He was very angry. He said, "You must worship God, not a statue. If you are sorry, come stand next to me." Some of the people were very sorry. But some of the people still wanted the golden calf. Moses destroyed the idol. God punished the people who didn't repent. Would you have stood next to Moses?

What to Do

✳ God is not happy when we worship other things instead of Him. Connect the dots to see what the Israelites worshipped instead of God.

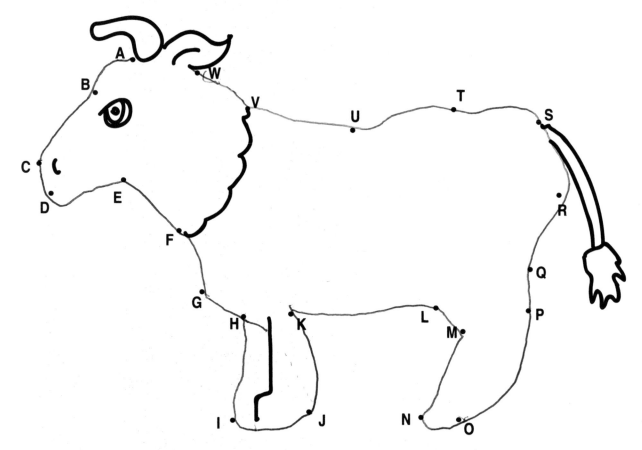

64

The Israelites Are Sorry

memory verse

Who can forgive sins but God alone? ~Luke 5:21

Snakes Everywhere (Numbers 21:4-9)

The Israelites grumbled at Moses as he led them to the land God promised. Some said, "We hate our food." Others said, "God does not help us." God had given the people good food. But they wanted something different to eat. They were tired of obeying God and following Moses. So God punished them. This time He sent snakes. Hundreds and hundreds of snakes! What would you do if you were there? "Run!" shouted the people. But they could not run from the snakes. There were too many. "Help us, Moses!" the people cried. God told Moses to make a big bronze snake. Moses obeyed God. He held the bronze snake high for everyone to see. Those who were sorry looked at the snake and did not die. God forgave them. Do you think they grumbled anymore?

What to Do

✳ There are a lot of snakes in the picture below. Can you count them?

7
Color the snakes.

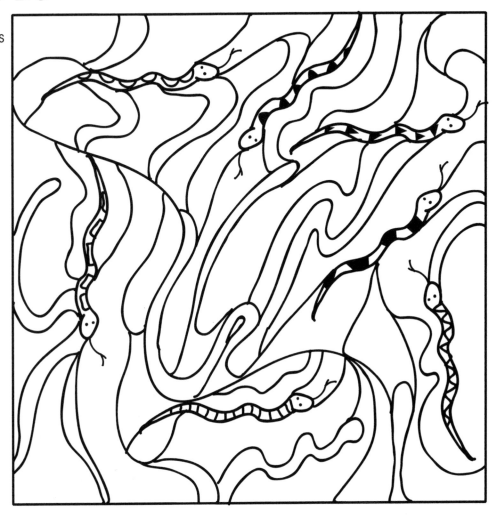

God Tells His People to Obey Him

memory verse
. . . .
Keep the commands of the Lord your God. ~Deuteronomy 4:2

Obeying God's Rules (Deuteronomy 4-6)

After God brought the Israelites out of Egypt they needed rules to govern their lives. We all need rules to live by, otherwise there is confusion and disorder. So God gave His people rules that would help them love and care for each other and worship Him.

What to Do

✱ Draw a line from the rule on the left to the picture that matches it on the right.

Obey Your Mother and Father.

Make God's Day Special!

Do Not Steal.

God Gives His People Rules

memory verse

These commandments that I give you today are to be upon your hearts.

~Deuteronomy 6:6

Follow God's Rules (Deuteronomy 5)

God wrote His rules on tablets of stone, but He wanted the people to keep the rules in their hearts. Keep God's laws in your hearts through good behavior and prayer.

What to Do

✱ Write the first letter of each object to finish this sentence starting with the hat and going to the right (clockwise).

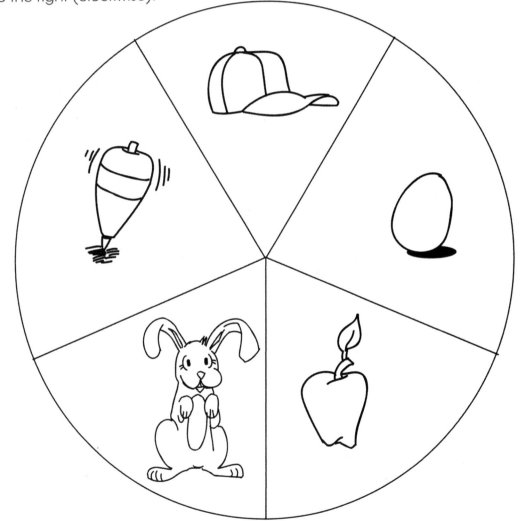

God's rules

are in your

heart

Obey and Don't Be Afraid

memory verse
. . . .
Be strong and courageous. ~Joshua 1:6

Joshua Led the Israelites (Joshua 1)

Moses led the people to a new land. But God wanted Moses to join Him in heaven. So God told Joshua to lead the people into the new land. Joshua was very young. God told him, "Don't be afraid. I will help you lead the people." Joshua obeyed God and led the people to the new land. God can help us to do things that we think we cannot do on our own.

What to Do

✳ Count the shapes in the picture and write the number of each in the blanks.

How many □'s? __4__

How many ○'s? __6__

How many △'s? __8__

God is Always There Maze

memory verse
....
The Lord your God will be with you wherever you go. ~Joshua 1:9

Leading the Israelites (Joshua 1)

Because the Israelites did not trust God, they had to follow Moses in the desert for 40 years. When Moses died, Joshua was sad. God chose Joshua to lead His people into the land that God had promised them. Joshua was feeling lonely. But God told Joshua, "I will not fail you or leave you. Be strong and courageous. Do not be afraid. The Lord your God will be with you wherever you go."

What to Do

✱ Follow the maze to help Joshua lead the people into the Promised Land. Trace the correct path with a pencil or crayon. Remember that God told Joshua not to be afraid. God promised Joshua that He would be with him wherever he went. God is with us wherever we go, too. When you feel lonely or afraid, remember that God is with you.

Promised Land

Joshua Fights a Battle

memory verse
....
Be strong and courageous. ~Joshua 1:6

The Walls of Jericho (Joshua 6)

God's people came to a big city with tall walls. God wanted His people to capture the city called Jericho. How could they do it? Jericho had a great army of soldiers. God told Joshua, "March around Jericho every day. On the seventh day, you must march seven times. After you march, blow your trumpets and shout." Joshua was a soldier. He was brave and fought hard. He had never fought a battle by just marching! But Joshua and the people did what God said. On the seventh day they marched seven times. Then they blew their trumpets and shouted. The walls of Jericho fell down! Joshua and his men marched in and took the city. Joshua was glad he trusted and obeyed God. We can obey God, too.

What to Do

✱ Cover up the bottom picture with a piece of paper. Look carefully at the top picture. When you are ready, cover the top picture and uncover the bottom one. Some of the parts are missing in the second picture. Circle the places where things are missing.

Jericho Falls

memory verse
. . . .
We will serve the Lord our God and obey him. ~Joshua 24:24

The Walls Fell Down (Joshua 6)

God told Joshua to march around Jericho every day. On the seventh day God said, "Tell the people to march around the city seven times. On the seventh time, blow the horns and shout loudly! The walls will fall down." Joshua and the people obeyed. The walls of Jericho came falling down. We can do incredible things if we obey God's commands!

What to Do

✱ God told the people to march around Jericho. In each row, color the people who are marching the same way.

God's Rules Are Good

memory verse

Keep my commands and follow them. I am the Lord. ~Leviticus 22:31

Keeping the Rules (Judges 2-3)

God's rules are for our good and protection. Which rules are easy to obey? Which ones are harder to obey?

What to Do

✳ Each of these children needs something to obey God's rules. Draw a line to the objects they need.

Hidden Message Puzzle

memory verse

I will make music to the Lord, the God of Israel. ~Judges 5:3

Praising God (Judges 5)

Deborah was wise, strong and brave. Deborah listened to God. Because Deborah obeyed God's plans for Israel, her people became stronger and stronger against their enemy. Deborah followed God, and the people followed Deborah. After they defeated King Jabin, a wicked king, the people sang a song thanking God for freeing them from an unkind enemy. They lived in peace for 40 years.

What to Do

✳ To discover Deborah's message, color red each space with a dot. Color the remaining sections in other bright colors.

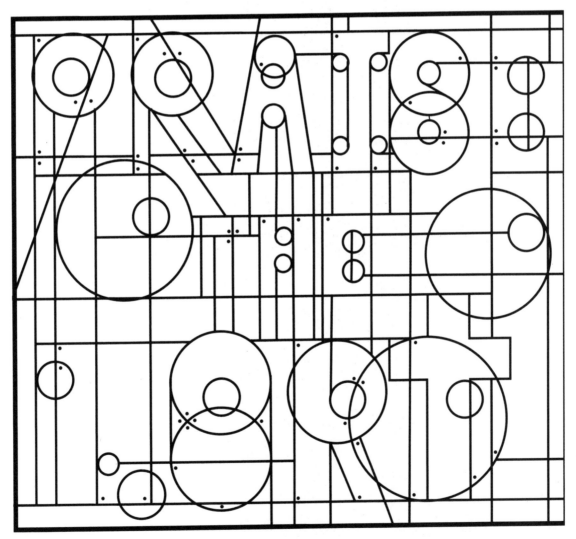

Gideon Defeats His Enemies

memory verse

A sword for the Lord and for Gideon! ~Judges 7:20

God Promises Victory (Judges 7:9-24)

The Lord spoke to Gideon in a dream. God promised to help Gideon defeat the Midianites.

What to Do

✳ Hidden in this picture are

6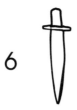

10 🔥

and 3 🫙

Can you find them?

A Boy of Great Strength

memory verse

[Samson] grew and the Lord blessed him. ~Judges 13:24

Samson is Special (Judges 13; 14:5-6)

Before Samson was born, an angel told his mother and father that Samson would be a very special son who would do the work of the Lord. The angel told Samson's parents to make sure he ate special foods and to never cut his hair. The Lord blessed Samson and made him really strong. He even killed a lion with his bare hands! God used Samson to save the Israelites from their enemies.

What to Do

✳ Both the lion and Samson are missing something. Can you guess what it is and draw it?

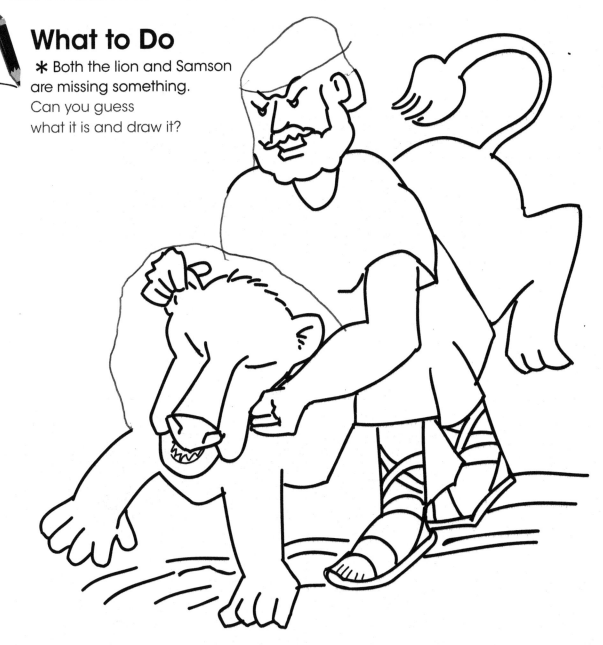

A Boy Shows Kindness

Samson and the Servant Boy (Judges 16:23-31)

The Philistines, Samson's enemies, found out the secret of his strength. They tricked Samson and cut off his hair. When he lost his hair he lost his strength. He became their prisoner. They poked out his eyes. But while he was in prison his hair grew back. One day the Philistines had a party in the temple of their idol. Samson asked a servant boy to lead him to the pillars of the temple. The boy felt sorry for the blind man and was kind to him. The boy helped Samson find the pillars. Samson asked God to give him his strength one more time. God answered his prayer. Samson pushed the pillars apart and the temple of the false god fell.

What to Do

✳ Help the servant boy lead Samson to the pillars.

A Faithful Friend

memory verse
....
Where you go I will go. ~Ruth 1:16

Together Forever (Ruth 1:16-17)

Naomi's husband and sons died. Naomi was all alone. But one of Naomi's sons had a lovely wife named Ruth. Ruth said she would always stay with Naomi. Naomi taught Ruth about God. Ruth learned to love and obey Naomi's God—the same God we worship today. We can share about our God with family and friends, too.

What to Do

✱ Ruth and Naomi were best friends. How many things can you find in the bottom picture that are different from the top one?

A Daughter-in-Law's Devotion

Ruth Insists on Staying With Naomi (Ruth 1:16-17)

Ruth said, "Don't urge me to leave you or to turn back from you. Where you go I will go, and where you stay I will stay. Your people will be my people and your God my God. Where you die I will die, and there I will be buried. May the Lord deal with me, be it ever so severely, if anything but death separates you and me."

What to Do

✳ There are many ways to show love and respect. Naomi's daughter-in-law Ruth was devoted to Naomi after their husbands died. She traveled with Naomi to Naomi's homeland. Read the Scripture to find clues to fill in the crossword puzzle.

Down
1. Many persons
4. Any object or matter
5. Divides into parts
7. At any time
8. To do business with
9. God
11. Placed in the ground after death
13. Remain in one place
16. Fifth month of the year

Across
2. Do not
3. Move to the rear
6. Harshly, intensely
8. To no longer live
10. Plead with
12. Great Creator
14. Answered
15. Go away from
17. To have died

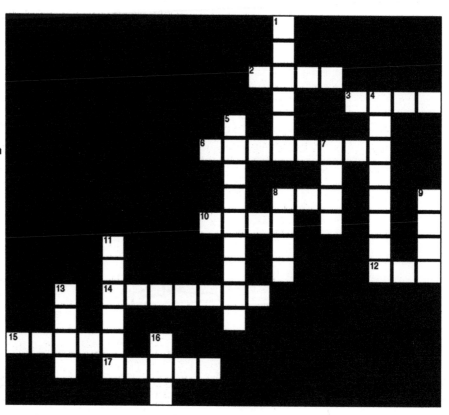

Gleaning Code

memory verse
....
May the Lord repay you for what you have done. May you be richly rewarded by the Lord, the God of Israel, under whose wings you have come to take refuge.   ~Ruth 2:12

Ruth Takes Care of Naomi (Ruth 2:1-23)

Naomi and Ruth were widows who lived in Moab. Naomi wanted to return to her country, Judah, because she had relatives there who would help her. Ruth, her daughter-in-law, went with her because she loved Naomi. It was harvest time and Ruth saw a field to glean. Gleaning, or picking up the leftovers, was the only way poor people could get food from the fields. Boaz, Naomi's relative, owned the field. He heard how Ruth left her family and country to take care of Naomi. Ruth found favor with Boaz. He encouraged her to glean only from his fields.

What to Do

✱ Solve the mystery code below by writing the letters that match the numbers.

Key

A	B	C	D	E
2	4	6	3	12
F	G	H	I	J
9	26	10	5	7
K	L	M	N	O
11	8	14	20	22
P	Q	R	S	T
17	15	18	16	24
U	V	W	X	Y	Z
30	19	23	21	40	27

24 22   26 8 12 2 20   14 12 2 20 16   40 22 30

__ __   __ __ __ __ __   __ __ __ __ __   __ __ __

16 10 2 18 12   4 12 6 2 30 16 12   40 22 30

__ __ __ __ __   __ __ __ __ __ __ __   __ __ __

6 2 18 12

__ __ __ __ .

A Mother Keeps Her Promise

memory verse
. . . .
Everyone has heard about your obedience, so I am full of joy. ~Romans 16:19

A Special Son (1 Samuel 1-2)

Hannah wanted a baby. Hannah promised that she would take her child to God's house, the tabernacle. God gave Hannah a special son. Hannah named him Samuel. When Samuel was old enough, Hannah kept her promise. She took him to the tabernacle. God rewards those who keep their promises to Him.

What to Do

✳ Help Hannah and Samuel get to the tabernacle by following the path.

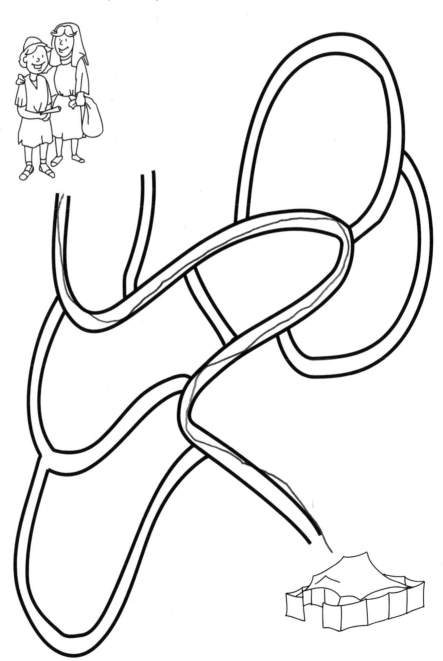

Easy or Hard

memory verse
I prayed for this child, and the Lord has granted me what I asked of him.
So now I give him to the Lord. ~1 Samuel 1:27–28

Hannah Gives Samuel to the Lord (1 Samuel 1:20-2:21)

Hannah prayed for years to have a baby. She promised God that if He gave her a son, she would give the son to Him. God answered her prayers and she gave birth to a son. She named him Samuel. When he was three years old, she took him to Eli, the temple priest, for him to raise. Hannah had kept her promise to God. Every year, she brought Samuel a robe that she had made.

What to Do

✱ Read each promise. Circle whether you think it would be an easy or hard promise to keep and write below it why you believe it would be easy or hard to do. Then unscramble the letters below to figure out the Bible verse.

1. I promise always to do my homework before watching TV.　　Easy　　　　Hard

_____

2. I promise never to be late.　　Easy　　　　Hard

_____

3. I promise always to keep my room clean.　　Easy　　　　Hard

_____

4. I promise never to say bad words.　　Easy　　　　Hard

_____

ROF　　ON　　TEMRAT　　WHO　　YAMN　　SROMPISE　　DGO

___　　__　　_____　　___　　____　　_____　　___

SHA　　DEAM　　YETH　　EAR　　"SEY"　　NI　　TRISHC

___　　____,　　____　　___　　___　　__　　_____.

2 Corinthians 1:20

Joyful Letters

memory verse
....
My heart rejoices in the Lord. ~1 Samuel 2:1

Hannah Praises God (1 Samuel 2:1-10)

It's easy to be happy when you have everything you want. But when you want something, it can be hard to wait for it. Hannah wanted a son but it took many years of praying before God answered her. When she had a son, she was so happy, she wanted to say "thank you" to God. So she began to praise Him. Hannah was happy and full of God's joy.

God gave us a special present, Jesus. He gives us joy!

What to Do

✱ At the bottom of the page, copy the letters from the lines that have a heart above them. Then read what the words say.

Disobedient Sons

memory verse

. . . .

They were disobedient and rebelled against [God]. ~Nehemiah 9:26

Good Behavior (1 Samuel 2:12-15)

Samuel grew up in the tabernacle. He was a good boy. Samuel obeyed Eli, the priest. Eli had two sons of his own but they did not obey their father. Eli's sons were disobedient. We should show God's love and always be obedient.

What to Do

* Draw a line to the pictures that show the opposite of Samuel's good actions.

Eli's Wicked Sons

memory verse

Eli's sons...had no regard for the Lord. ~1 Samuel 2:12

A Big Difference (1 Samuel 2:12-17; 22-25)

Eli's sons were very wicked boys. They paid no attention to their father's instructions. They made fun of the ceremonies of the temple and ate the sacrifices. But Samuel was never affected by these boys. He continued to grow in favor with the Lord. We can still follow God even when people around us may not be following Him.

What to Do

✱ Samuel was very different from Eli's sons. Circle the picture of the boy in each row who is following God's rules.

Samuel Obeys God's Call

memory verse
. . . .
Listen to what I say to you. ~Ezekiel 2:8

Samuel Listens (1 Samuel 3)

Samuel loved God. Samuel also loved God's house. One night God talked to Samuel. God told Samuel some things He planned to do. Samuel listened and obeyed God. We should listen to God, too.

What to Do

✳ Hidden in this picture are an oil lamp, a water pitcher, a lamb, a scroll and a patched robe. Can you find them?

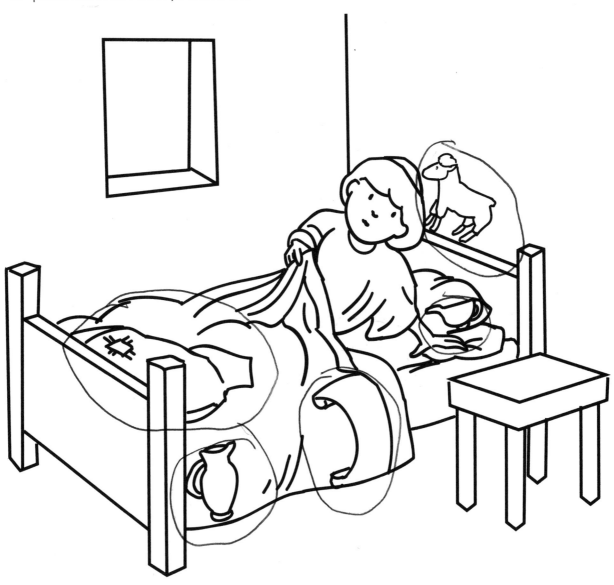

Finding God's Word

memory verse
. . . .
The Lord called Samuel. ~1 Samuel 3:4

God Calls Samuel
to Be a Prophet (1 Samuel 3:1-21)

Hannah, Samuel's mother, took him to the temple when he was just 3 years old. Eli, the temple priest, raised Samuel to love and worship God. When Samuel was still a boy, God began to tell Samuel many things. As Samuel grew, God continued to teach Samuel important rules. Samuel listened to and obeyed God.

What to Do

❋ Follow the path to find letters that will make a special word. Write the letters from the path on the blanks below

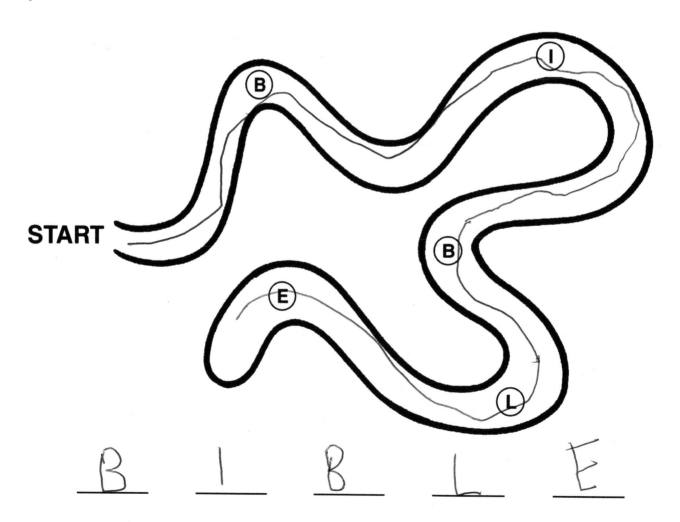

START

B   I   B   L   E

Interference in My Life

memory verse

Then the Lord called Samuel. Samuel answered, "Here I am." ~1 Samuel 3:4

God Speaks to Samuel (1 Samuel 3:1-21)

Hannah's son Samuel lived with Eli, the temple priest, who taught him about God. Samuel loved and trusted God. One night, Samuel heard his name called. He got out of bed, went to Eli and asked him what he wanted. Eli told Samuel that he hadn't called him and sent him back to bed. This happened several more times before Eli realized it was God calling Samuel. He told Samuel to say, "Speak, for your servant is listening." God used Samuel as a prophet.

What to Do

✱ It is easy to say you will study God's Word, but too often, things and activities interfere, as you will see when you travel through the maze below. Complete the maze by choosing the best start point to get to the Bible.

Samuel Finds Israel a King

memory verse

The Lord answered, "Listen to them and give them a king." ~1 Samuel 8:22

Obeying a King (1 Samuel 8)

Obeying just God wasn't enough for the Israelites. The people wanted a king to obey. God told Samuel to find the people a king. Samuel warned the people that a king would be hard to obey. Do you think it would be hard to obey a king?

What to Do

* How many crowns can you find in this picture? Color them.

Find the Donkeys

memory verse

Before I was born the Lord called me. ~Isaiah 49:1

Samuel Listens to God (1 Samuel 9)

God spoke to Samuel when he was still a young boy. But that wasn't the only time God spoke to him. Samuel grew up to be a great prophet of God. One day, God spoke to Samuel and said, "Tomorrow a stranger will visit you. He is the one who will become king of Israel."

The next day, a man named Saul was looking for his father's lost donkeys. He and his servant looked everywhere, but still no donkeys! So Saul stopped at Samuel's house to see if Samuel knew where the donkeys were. Then Samuel knew Saul would become the first king of God's people.

What to Do

✻ Where are the donkeys for which Saul and his servant were looking? See if you can find five donkeys in the picture. Then you can color the picture.

God Chooses David

memory verse
....
The Lord looks at the heart. ~1 Samuel 16:7

Hearts for God (1 Samuel 16:1-13)

The Lord told Samuel to go to Bethlehem to find the next king of Israel. Samuel saw Jesse's sons. One by one Samuel looked at each young man and prayed, "Is this the new king, Lord?" The Lord told Samuel, "Do not look at their faces. The Lord looks at the heart." Jesse's youngest son, David, was taking care of the sheep. When Samuel saw David, the Lord told him this boy would be the new king of Israel. David had a good heart and loved God.

What to Do

✳ David loved God with all his heart. How many hearts can you count in this picture? 13

David Serves Saul

memory verse
....
Love your enemies. ~Matthew 5:44

David Loved King Saul (1 Samuel 16:14-23;18:10-12)

King Saul had lost God's approval. There were many nights when he could not sleep. Saul asked his helpers to find someone to play music for him. David could play the harp. When Saul could not sleep, David played his harp softly for him. Saul became jealous of David. One day as David played his harp, Saul threw a spear at him. But David continued to love Saul and never became angry at the king.

What to Do

* Color this picture, then circle the pictures below that rhyme with LOVE.

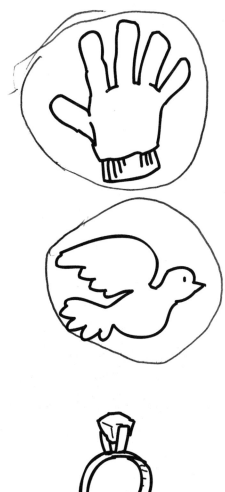

91

A Shepherd Boy

memory verse
. . . .
The Lord is my shepherd. ~Psalm 23:1

Lions and Bears (1 Samuel 17:34–37)

David was a shepherd boy. He watched after his father's sheep day and night. David was a very good shepherd. One day while David watched the sheep, a hungry bear came out of the woods and grabbed a lamb. David wasn't afraid. He killed the bear and saved his sheep. Another time a lion attacked his sheep. David grabbed the lion by its hair and killed it. David wasn't afraid because he knew God would help him protect his sheep. David trusted God to watch over him just as he watched over his sheep.

What to Do

* With God's help, David killed a lion and a bear. Can you find the lions and bears in this picture?

Help with Fighting Giants

memory verse
....
David said to Saul, "...Your servant will go and fight him." ~1 Samuel 17:32

David Kills Goliath (1 Samuel 17)

David and his brothers lived in Bethlehem. They raised sheep. Three of David's brothers went off to fight against the Philistines. David's father sent him to check on his brothers. While he was there, David heard the men talking about a giant called Goliath. Goliath fought with the Philistines. No one could defeat him. David told King Saul that he would fight him. Using only a slingshot, David killed Goliath by hitting him in the head with a stone.

What to Do

✱ Write the answer to each question. Then write the numbered letters on the lines below in the correct order to find out what Saul said to David before he went to battle against Goliath. Then cross out the last word in the sentence and put your name instead.

1. Who killed the giant? __ __ __ __ __
                 12 3   5

2. What was the giant's name? __ __ __ __ __ __ __
                 1 10   17 7

3. Who was the king? __ __ __ __
               21 9

4. What did David use as a weapon? __ __ __ __ __ __ __ __
                 16 4   2

5. Where did he live with his brothers? __ __ __ __ __ __ __ __ __
               13   6 18   14   8

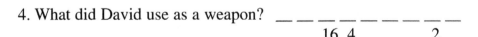

__ __   __ __ __   __ __ __   __ __ R __
1 2   3 4 5   6 7 8   9 10 11 12

__ __   W __ __ __   Y O __.
13 14   15 16 17 18   19 20 21

Obedience Kills a Giant

memory verse

Your servant will go and fight [Goliath]. ~1 Samuel 17:32

David Fights the Giant (1 Samuel 17)

When David was a little boy, he wanted to fight Goliath, a giant. The grown-up soldiers laughed at him. So did the king. "How could a small boy fight a giant?" they asked. "God will help me!" said David. And He did!

What to Do

✳ Find seven things in the bottom picture that are different from the top one.

Good Friends

memory verse
Submit to one another. ~Ephesians 5:21

Being a Friend (1 Samuel 18:1-4)

Jonathan knew that David obeyed and trusted God. He knew that God helped David kill Goliath. Jonathan liked that David followed God so he and David became best friends. He was able to help David and David helped him, too. Submitting means that we are nice to our friends and family. It can be hard to let someone else have their way when we want something different. What are some times when it might be hard to go along with what someone else wants?

What to Do

✱ What do good friends do? Write the first letter of each picture in the space below it.

David Shows Mercy

Treating Others Kindly (1 Samuel 24)

King Saul didn't always love God. Soon he became selfish and a bad king. He grew jealous of David because he was a great soldier. David killed more Philistines than Saul. The people loved David more than Saul. Many times Saul tried to kill David. One day Saul set out to look for David. Saul came to a cave. He went inside to rest. David and his men were hiding far back in the cave. David crept up and cut off a piece of Saul's robe. David could have killed Saul and not have to worry anymore about Saul chasing him. But David decided to show mercy and let Saul go. God likes it when we are kind and merciful to others.

What to Do

✳ Write the first letter of the picture. Then read the message.
The first letter is done for you.

David showed Saul...

_M_ _e_ _r_ _c_ _y_

Kindness to a Crippled Boy

memory verse

· ·

The fruit of the spirit is...kindness. ~Galatians 5:22

Searching for Kindness (2 Samuel 4:4; 9:1-13)

A terrible thing happened to a little boy named Mephibosheth, who was Jonathan's son and Saul's grandson. One day a messenger came running saying, "Jonathan and King Saul are dead." They had died in a battle. Mephibosheth's nurse was scared. She grabbed the little boy quickly, carrying him in her arms. But as she ran, she dropped the boy. His feet were badly hurt. Mephibosheth could never walk or run like other children. Jonathan was David's best friend before he died. David had promised to be kind to Jonathan's children. When David became king, he sent for the boy and loved him as if he were his own son. David kept his promise and showed kindness to Mephibosheth.

What to Do

✱ Hidden in this picture are the letters that spell KINDNESS
Cross them out as you find them.

Showing Kindness

memory verse

Love is kind. ~1 Corinthians 13:4

David Is Kind (2 Samuel 9)

King David's best friend was Jonathan, King Saul's son. When the two were young men, they promised they would always be friends. David also promised Jonathan that he would always take care of Jonathan's family.

Jonathan was killed in a battle with the Philistines. David instructed his men to find Jonathan's family. They found Jonathan's son, Mephibosheth, who was not able to walk because of an accident when he was a baby.

"Don't be afraid," David told him. "Your father was my best friend ... I will give you all the land that belonged to Saul, your grandfather. I will give you everything you need."

"Thank you, King David," Mephibosheth said. "Thank you for your kindness."

What to Do

✱ When we are kind, it makes three people smile: you, the one to whom you showed kindness and God. Color the picture using red, blue, green, yellow, black and tan as indicated by the color key on the side.

Love is kind. 1 Corinthians 13:4

1. red
2. blue
3. green
4. yellow
5. black
6. tan

Kind King David

memory verse
. . . .
Be kind and compassionate to one another.   ~Ephesians 4:32

King David Shows
Kindness to Mephibosheth (Genesis 4:1-2)

David became king of Israel after Saul died. He was a good king. He helped his people. David's best friend was Jonathan. Jonathan died in a battle. His son Mephibosheth had no place to live. Jonathan's son was crippled and walked with crutches. David wanted to show kindness to Mephibosheth. David took care of the boy. Mephibosheth went to live in the palace with David. Do you think King David was kind?

What to Do

✳ Look at the pictures in each row. Color the pictures in each row that look the same as the first picture in that row.

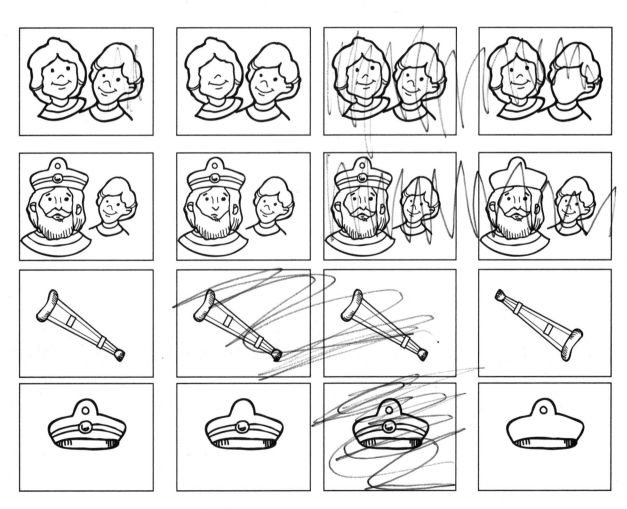

Friends Forever

 memory verse

A friend loves at all times.   ~Proverbs 17:17

David Loved Jonathan's Son (2 Samuel 9:1-13)

David loved Jonathan very much. Even after Jonathan died, David wanted to show how much he loved his friend. So he took care of Jonathan's son Mephibosheth, a crippled boy. We can always do nice things for our friends, whether they are big actions like David did or just little things like sharing.

What to Do

✻ The five objects below are hidden in this picture. Can you find them?

Training a King

memory verse

Solomon...shall be king. ~1 Kings 1:30

David Has a Son (2 Samuel 12:24 and 1 Kings 1:28-30)

After David became king, he married Bathsheba. They had a son and named him Solomon. King David had other children, but he promised Bathsheba that Solomon would become the king when he died. While Solomon was growing up, King David taught him many things. Most importantly, he taught Solomon to worship and obey God. With God on their side, the king's army could fight their enemies.

You can worship God by praying and singing to Him. God is pleased when we worship Him. All you need to know about God is in the Bible.

What to Do

✳ Connect the dots to reveal the most important thing Solomon would need to know.

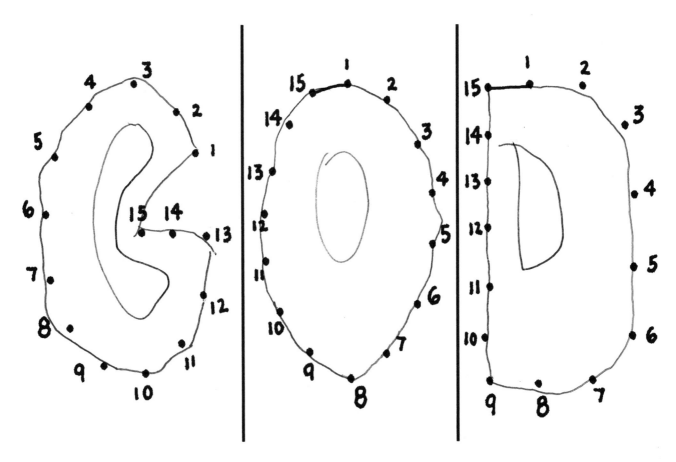

Where Can I Worship God?

memory verse
. . . .
Solomon built the temple and completed it. ~1 Kings 6:14

Solomon Builds
a Temple for God (1 Kings 2-7)

King David taught his son Solomon how to be a king with whom God would be pleased. He instructed Solomon to obey God's laws so he would be a good example to the people. After King David died, Solomon became the new king. Four years later, Solomon began building a temple for God. It was to be a special place for worship. The temple took seven years to build. When it was finished, King Solomon said a special prayer of thanks to God.

What to Do
✱ To worship God means to love and show honor to Him. Can you think of other places to worship God? Unscramble the letters in each word to find places you can worship God.

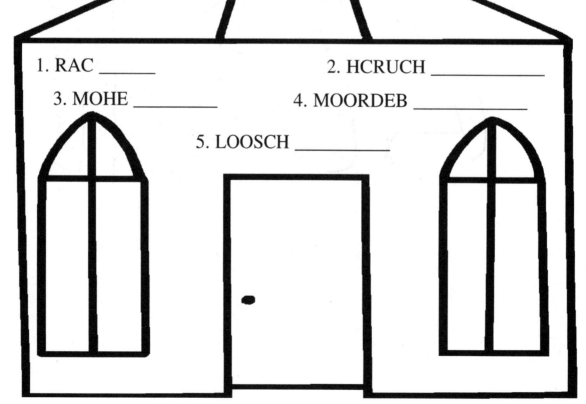

1. RAC _____

2. HCRUCH _____

3. MOHE _____

4. MOORDEB _____

5. LOOSCH _____

A Wise King

Solomon Asks for Wisdom (1 Kings 3:7-9)

"Now, O Lord my God, you have made your servant king in place of my father David. But I am only a little child and do not know how to carry out my duties. Your servant is here among the people you have chosen, a great people, too numerous to count or number. So give your servant a discerning heart to govern your people and to distinguish between right and wrong. For who is able to govern this great people of yours?"

What to Do

* Solomon could have asked the Lord for anything, just as we can. He didn't ask for material things, however. He asked for something else. Use the clues from this Scripture describing his request, then fill in the crossword puzzle.

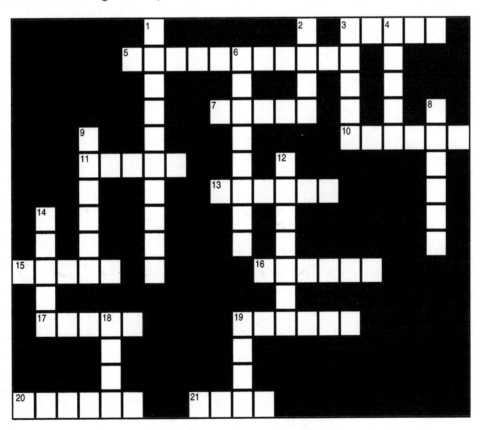

Down
1. To perceive with the mind
2. A ruler of a country
3. Son or daughter
4. Proper, correct
6. Many
8. Many persons
9. Selected
12. One who serves another
14. Not correct
18. Having enough ability
19. God

Across
3. Transport
5. Recognize as distinct
7. In the group or company of
10. Tasks or assignments
11. Where love is felt
13. Guide
15. To name one by one for a total
16. Male parent
17. Remarkable; outstanding
19. Small
20. A sum or quantity
21. Created

Building God's House

memory verse

Let us go to the house of the Lord. ~Psalm 122:1

A Special House (1 Kings 2–7)

King Solomon loved God. He wanted to show God how much he loved Him. So King Solomon decided to build a special house for God where the people could talk to Him. Solomon built a beautiful house for God. Then Solomon told all of the people, "Come worship at God's house." God loves when we come to church and worship Him.

What to Do

✴ First help the construction workers and the musician find God's house. Then help Solomon and the people find their way to worship there.

Bad Friends

memory verse
. . . .
Bad company corrupts good character. ~1 Corinthians 15:33

In the Way (1 Kings 11:1-13)

Solomon didn't always make wise choices. As his kingdom grew, Solomon gained many friends. Some of these friends worshipped idols and not God. Solomon allowed these friends to worship idols in his land. Soon all the people forgot God and began worshiping idols. Solomon allowed idols and his friends to come between him and God. We should not allow anything to come between us and following God.

What to Do

✱ Circle what is BETWEEN Solomon and the temple in each picture.

105

God Takes Care of Elijah

memory verse
He cares for those who trust in Him. ~Nahum 1:7

Elijah Trusts God (1 Kings 17:1-5)

A wicked king ruled Israel. He encouraged the people to worship idols. God told Elijah to go deep into the woods because He was going to punish Israel. For many years there would be no rain in the land. Elijah trusted and obeyed God. He had no food to eat, but God sent Elijah food in a special way.

What to Do

* Color all the spaces with dots BLACK.

Color the space with a star YELLOW.

Color the empty spaces LIGHT BLUE.

How did God feed Elijah?

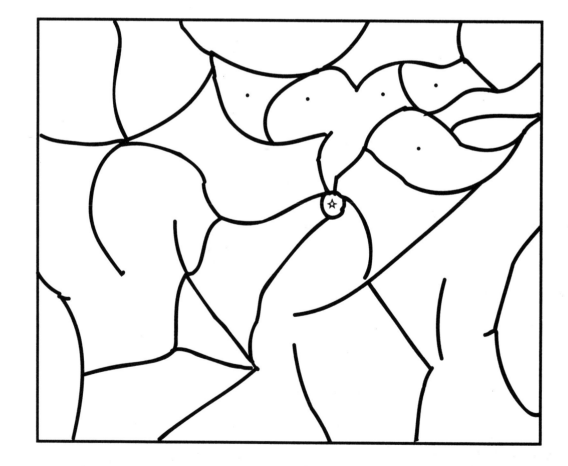

Ravens Feed Elijah

memory verse
. . . .
The Lord will watch over your coming and going both now and forevermore.

~Psalm 121:8

Special Delivery (1 Kings 17:1-6)

Elijah was a prophet of God. A prophet was God's helper. Prophets told people what God said and they did great miracles. Because the people were very bad, Elijah told them that God was angry. There would be no rain for a few years. Without rain, crops would die and there would be no food in the land. But God took care of Elijah. He told the prophet to go to a special place near a river. Elijah went to the place God said. Each day God sent ravens. The ravens brought bread and meat to Elijah morning and night. God took care of Elijah during the time of no rain or food. Do you think Elijah was thankful?

What to Do

✱ Connect the dots to see what brought Elijah food each morning and night.

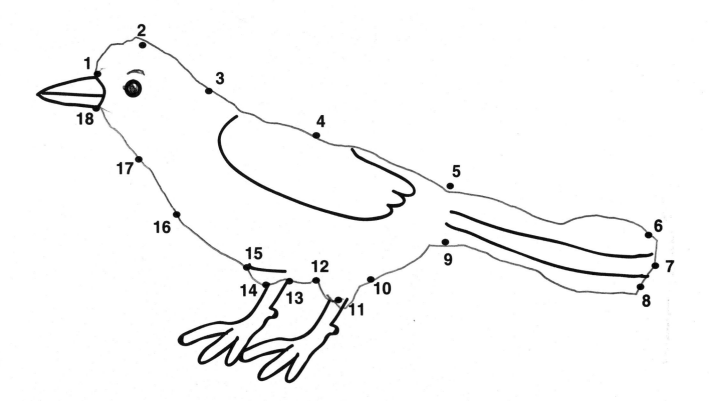

The True God

memory verse

The Lord — he is God! ~1 Kings 18:39

God Sent Fire (1 Kings 18:16–45)

Some foolish people believed that Baal was the true God. But Elijah knew differently. One day he decided to prove who was the true God. So he built an altar and put meat on it. He told the foolish people to ask Baal to send fire down on the altar. Nothing happened. Elijah poured water on the altar. He prayed and asked God to send fire. God sent fire from heaven on the altar. Our God is stronger than any fake idol that people create.

What to Do

✳ Can you draw an altar? Trace over the dots to fill in the boxes in the grid, then look at the example and draw what is missing in the empty boxes.

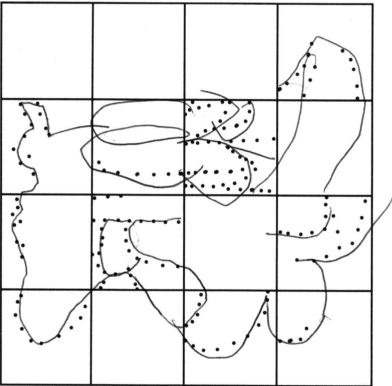

Elisha Follows Elijah

memory verse
. . . .
I will keep your law and obey it with all my heart. ~Psalm 119:34

Seeking Knowledge (1 Kings 19:19-21; 2 Kings 2)

The prophet Elijah had a follower named Elisha. Elisha wanted to learn all about following God. Elisha wanted to understand all he could about God's power so he could teach the people to obey.

What to Do

✳ How many things in the top picture are different from the one below it?

The Prophet's Quiz

A Pouting King (1 Kings 21)

King Ahab was out walking one day when he found a beautiful vineyard. Many grapes hung on the vines. When King Ahab tasted the fruit, he knew he had never tasted such delicious grapes. He asked the owner of the vineyard, Naboth, if he could buy it. Naboth told him no because it was an inheritance from his family. King Ahab went home and pouted. He already had much more than he needed, but he pouted because he could not have even more.

What to Do

✳ There was a prophet who told King Ahab what a greedy man he was. Work the puzzle to find out the name of the prophet. Write the letters in the blanks to spell out the answer.

_e_ A letter between D and G, the one that rhymes with "bee."

_L_ A letter before M but after J, the one that rhymes with "bell."

_i_ A letter that's a vowel, the one that rhymes with "pie."

_j_ A letter after G, the one after "blue" in a type of bird.

_a_ A letter before C, the one that rhymes with what horses eat.

_h_ A letter after F, but before J, the one that begins the word for what you have on your head.

Learning a Lesson in Respect

memory verse

Show proper respect to everyone. ~1 Peter 2:17

No Respect (2 Kings 2:23-24)

God sent Elisha to preach His Word. God wanted all of His people to respect and listen to Elisha. One day as Elisha was traveling, a group of boys began to make fun of Elisha. They called, "Go on, baldhead! Go on, baldhead!" They laughed and made fun of God's servant. Elisha asked God to help him. Suddenly, two big bears came out of the woods. The bears snarled and growled at the boys. Forty-two of the boys in the group were hurt. God taught them an important lesson about making fun of people.

What to Do

✱ Draw a line from the children who are not behaving God's way to those who are.

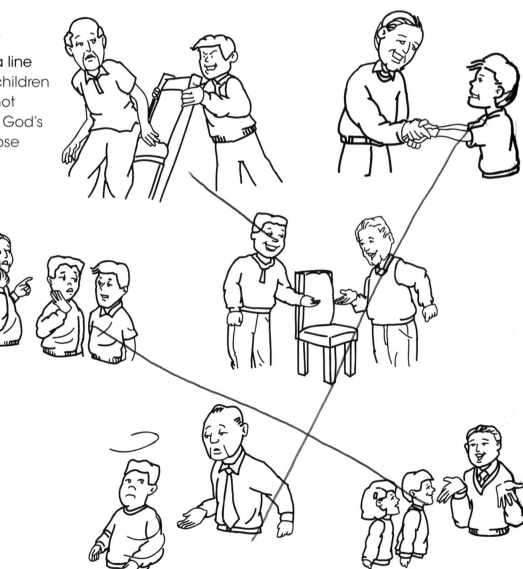

A Widow Keeps Her Sons

memory verse
. . . .
He saved them from their distress. ~Psalm 107:13

Jars of Plenty (2 Kings 4:1-7)

A long time ago there was a widow with two sons. When her husband died, he owed a lot of money. A mean man wanted to collect the money from the woman. She told him, "I can't pay you. I have no money." All she had was one small pot of oil. So the man told her, "I will return. If you cannot pay me, I will take your two sons as my slaves." Elisha heard of the woman's trouble. He told her to collect as many jars as she could find. Then Elisha told her to pour the oil into the jars. It kept pouring and pouring and pouring. When all of the jars were full the oil stopped. The woman sold the oil and paid her debt. There was enough money left that she never had to worry about losing her sons again.

What to Do

✱ The widow and her two sons filled many jars with oil. Can you count the jars in this picture?

Hospitality for a Prophet

memory verse

. . . .

Share with God's people who are in need. ~Romans 12:13

Showing Hospitality (2 Kings 4:8-10)

The prophet Elisha traveled throughout the countryside helping the people. One day he went to Shunem. There a kind woman saw that Elisha needed a place to stay. So she asked her husband to build a special room for Elisha to stay whenever he came that way. In return, Elisha promised her that the Lord would give her a son. She probably raised the boy to have a servant heart like her own. Whenever Elisha came, the boy would have served him like his mother did. Sharing is always right.

What to Do

✱ Draw a line from the boy to the things he may have used to show Elisha kindness..

Helping Her Master

memory verse
. . . .
Love one another. ~1 John 3:23

Seven Times (2 Kings 5:1-16)

One of the children taken from Jerusalem to Babylon was a little girl. She lived in the house of a man named Naaman, a captain in the Syrian army. One day Naaman became very sick. He had leprosy, which caused bad sores all over his body. The servant girl felt sorry for her master, even though he had taken her from her family. She told him about the prophet Elisha who could help him. Elisha told Naaman to wash seven times in the muddy Jordan River. When Naaman did this, he was totally healed. He was healed because of a servant girl's love for others.

What to Do

✳ The little servant girl sent Naaman to Elisha. Elisha told Naaman to bathe seven times in the River Jordan. Seven is an important number in the Bible. Hidden in this picture are seven number 7s. Can you find them?

Obeying the Law of God

memory verse

Oh, how I love your law! ~Psalm 119:97

A Surprise Treasure (2 Kings 22; 23:1-25)

Once an 8-year-old boy became the king of Judah. His name was Josiah. While Josiah was king, the people began to do bad things. They worshipped idols instead of God. The priest, Hilkiah, taught Josiah the ways of the Lord. Josiah became a good king. He ordered that the temple of the Lord be repaired and the idols torn down. While the workers repaired the temple they found a copy of God's law. Josiah was excited. He ordered the people to obey God's law. God was very pleased with King Josiah.

What to Do

✱ King Josiah found something very special. Connect the dots to see what it was.

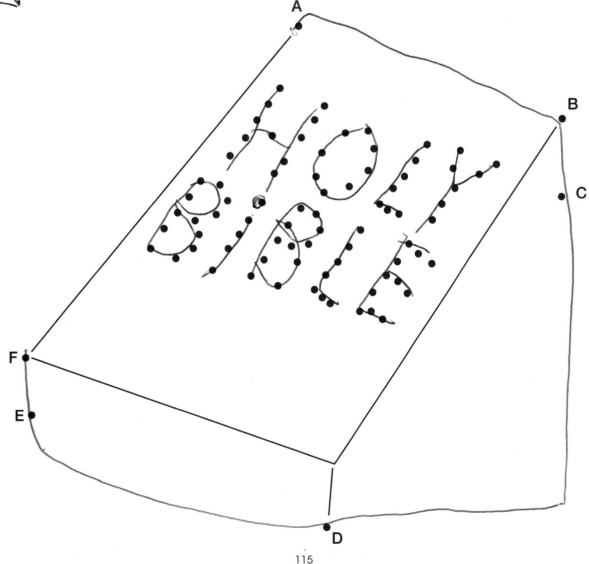

King Josiah Finds God's Word

 memory verse
....
Your word is a lamp to my feet and a light for my path. ~Psalm 119:105

God's Word Guides Us (2 Kings 22; 2 Chronicles 34:14-33)

King Josiah commanded that the temple of the Lord be repaired. While the men were working, they found something really special — the Word of the Lord. They found the commandments that God had given His people. When King Josiah read the scrolls, he realized that God's Word told the people how to live in a way that was good and right. He was sad because the people had been disobeying God's Word. The Bible helps us know how to obey God today.

 ## What to Do

✱ Just like a lamp or flashlight shows us where to walk in the dark, the Bible lights our paths by showing us how to love and obey God. Write the words for the pictures to finish the memory verse.

   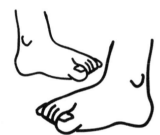

Your Word is a _____ **to my** _____ **and**

a _____ **for my** _____ **.**

Thanking God

memory verse
. . . .
Give thanks to the Lord, call on his name. ~1 Chronicles 16:8

Responding to God's Love (1 Chronicles 13, 15 and 16)

God's Word was kept in a very special place called the Ark of the Covenant. For a long time the ark was not in Jerusalem where the people worshipped. So King David brought the ark back to its rightful place. The people were so happy, because now they had the Word of God near them. As the ark was carried into Jerusalem, the people shouted praises of thanksgiving to God. King David wrote a special song thanking God for the return of the ark. We can thank God that His Word is close to us, too.

What to Do

* Write the first letter of each object in the wheel below, starting with the top, and going clockwise to fill in the blank.

Give _____ to the Lord!

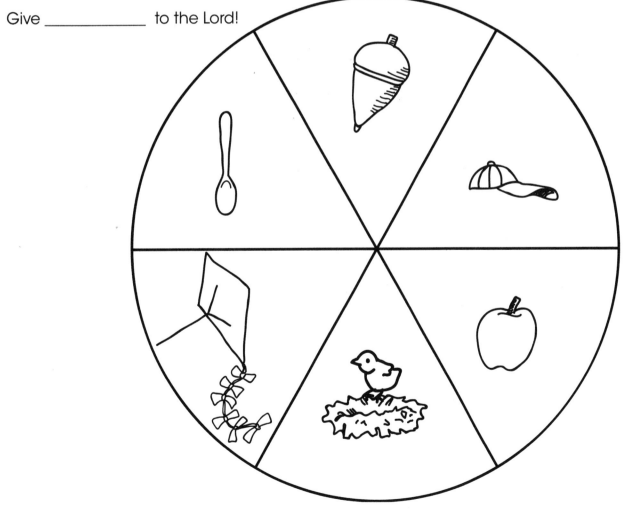

117

Worshipping in God's House

memory verse

Come, let us bow down in worship. ~Psalm 95:6

Praying in God's House (2 Chronicles 3:1-17; 5:12-14)

King Solomon loved God. To show God how much he loved Him, Solomon built a special house. This house was called a temple. People came to God's house. There they worshipped God. They talked to God. They sang songs of praise to God. God's house was very beautiful. The people loved singing songs about God. They loved praying to God in His house. Do you like to pray and sing in God's house, too?

What to Do

* There are four things that don't belong in this picture. Can you find them?

Hezekiah Repents of His Pride

memory verse
....
Hezekiah repented of the pride of his heart. ~2 Chronicles 32:26

Hezekiah Obeys Again (2 Chronicles 32:24-33)

Hezekiah did many great things to restore Israel. However, Hezekiah soon became prideful and forgot the kindness the Lord had shown him. God was angry with Hezekiah's disobedience. But then the king repented of his pride. God was happy that Hezekiah obeyed Him again.

What to Do

✱ In the squares going down write the name of the picture above. Then read across to fill in the blank below.

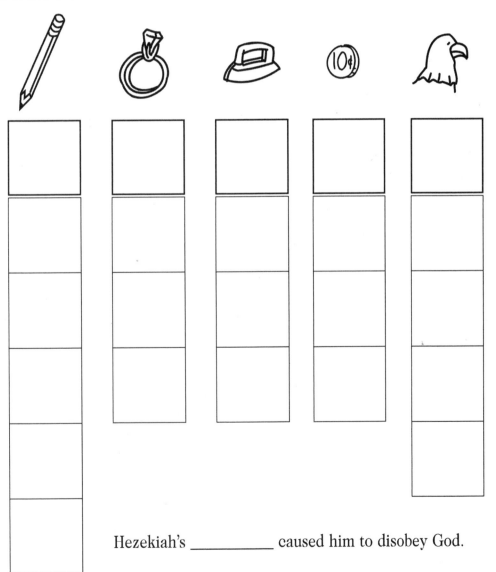

Hezekiah's _____ caused him to disobey God.

Repairing the Walls

memory verse

Let us rebuild the wall. ~Nehemiah 2:17

Good as New (Nehemiah 1-2)

Jerusalem was a beautiful city. But the Babylonian soldiers tore it down. The walls were in terrible condition for years. Nehemiah said to the king, "Let me go and repair the walls of Jerusalem." The king liked Nehemiah and agreed. Nehemiah worked hard to obey God and rebuild the city. God was pleased. God expects us to work hard to obey Him.

What to Do

✸ Draw a line from each stone to where it fits in the wall.

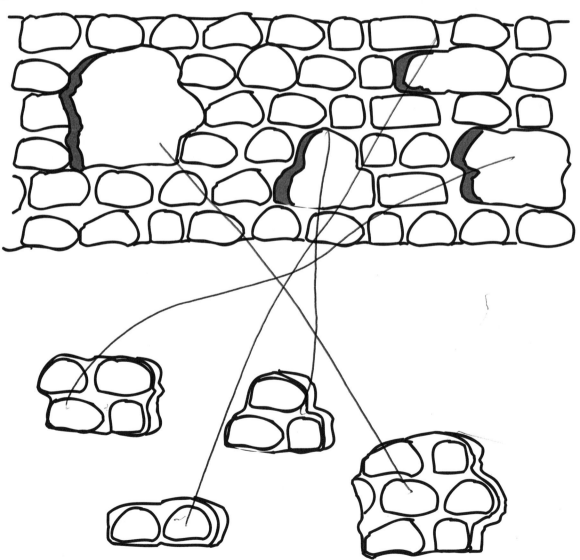

Nehemiah Looks at the Walls of Jerusalem

memory verse

We have not obeyed the commands, decrees and laws. ~Nehemiah 1:7

A Sad Ride (Nehemiah 2:11-16)

Nehemiah was very sad when he heard that the walls of Jerusalem were torn down. He confessed the disobedience of the people. When he went to Jerusalem, he rode on a horse around the city to see how much damage had occurred.

What to Do

✳ Nehemiah has lost his horse. Can you help him find it? Color it in when you do.

The Secret of Strength Hidden Message

memory verse
. . . .
This day is holy unto the Lord your God; mourn not, nor weep. ~Nehemiah 8:9

Discovering a Secret (Nehemiah 8:8-12)

When the Israelites heard the book of God's law read, they cried because they felt guilty for not obeying God. Nehemiah told them, "This is a day to be happy, because you have understood God's Book. Go and make feasts and celebrate. Give to the poor who have nothing to eat." So the people had a great celebration. Then they confessed their sins and began doing what was right.

What to Do

✳ How did the Israelites find strength to do many difficult things in serving God? Nehemiah told them a secret for finding strength. Solve the puzzle to discover his secret. Using a light color, color all the squares with a dot in the bottom right. With a dark color, color all the squares with a dot in the top left.

Use a light color for squares like this:

Use a dark color for squares like this:

Esther Saves Her People

memory verse

A woman who fears the Lord is to be praised. ~Proverbs 31:30

Esther is Brave (Esther 1–9)

The king wanted a beautiful wife. He told his servants to find every lovely girl in the country. He chose Esther to become his queen. He loved Esther very much. Haman was one of the king's helpers. But he was a very wicked man. He wanted to kill all of the Jewish people. He tricked the king into killing these people. The king did not know that Esther was Jewish. Esther went to the king and told him that she was a Jew. She did not want her people to die. The king became angry. He realized he had been tricked. He loved Esther and would not kill her. The king punished Haman and saved the Jewish people. Do you think that God had a special plan for Esther to become queen?

What to Do

✱ Words from the story appear on the left side of this page below. Look at the picture on the right. Match each sentence with a picture. Draw a line between them.

Who Said That?   **I Said That!**

I hate the Jewish people!

Esther

Please don't kill me!

King

I love you and I will save you.

Haman

Outside-Inside Plans

memory verse
The king was attracted to Esther… so he set a royal crown on her head and made her queen. ~Esther 2:17

Esther Becomes Queen (Esther 2:1-18)

Esther was raised by her cousin Mordecai because her parents had died. Both of them were Jews. They worshipped only God. King Xerxes needed a new queen, so all the young women were brought before him. Esther was one of the women. The king picked Esther because she was beautiful. Mordecai instructed Esther not to tell she was Jewish.

What to Do

✱ Why is it easy to judge people by how they look on the outside? How can people show that they have a heart for God? You can choose to have a heart for God.

Read each sentence and circle whether it is true or false. If it is false, write the letter under KING XERXES. If the sentence is true, write the letter under GOD.

Then unscramble the letters in each word to see what each one saw in Esther.

	T	**F**
1. Esther was old.	A	B
2. She was raised by a cousin.	H	E
3. Mordecai was her father.	S	T
4. Esther's parents had died.	E	L
5. The king wanted two new queens.	F	E
6. The king's name was Saul.	O	Y
7. Mordecai told Esther to say she was Jewish so she'd be selected.	T	U
8. Esther worshipped only God.	A	B
9. All young women were brought before the king.	T	M
10. Esther was chosen because she was beautiful.	R	N
11. Mordecai worshipped Esther.	Z	A

King Xerxes   God

— — — — —   — — — — —

A Beautiful Queen Obeys

memory verse
....
I have obeyed my Father's commands. ~John 15:10

God Works Through Esther (Esther 2-6)

The king needed a new queen. He picked Esther. Esther was beautiful. The king gave her beautiful clothes and jewelry. She was a successful queen because she allowed God to use her. God can use each of us if we give Him control of our lives.

What to Do

✱ Esther is getting ready to see the king. Draw a line from Esther to the clothes she might have worn to visit the king.

Esther Obeys
Mordecai's Instruction

memory verse

Whoever gives heed to instruction prospers. ~Proverbs 16:20

For the Sake of the People (Esther 2-6)

Esther was really frightened when she heard what her older cousin Mordecai wanted her to say to the king. No one was allowed to go before the king unless invited. Esther was afraid that the king might have her put to death. But for the sake of her people, she decided to do everything Mordecai told her and talked to the king. The king listened to her.

What to Do

✱ There are many people waiting to see the king. Look for Queen Esther and circle her, then color the picture.

Hearing the Truth Maze

memory verse

Mordecai found out about the plot and told Queen Esther, who in turn reported it to the king. . ~Esther 2:22

Esther and Mordecai Save the King

(Esther 2:19–23)

King Xerxes chose Esther to be his queen because she was beautiful. The king didn't know that she was Jewish. Her cousin Mordecai told her not to tell anyone that she was a Jew. One day while Mordecai was near the king's gate, he overheard two men talking. They worked for King Xerxes. They were planning to kill him! Mordecai told Queen Esther, who told the king. The king's life was saved because he knew what the two men were planning. God would use Queen Esther and Mordecai to save many more people.

What to Do

* Mordecai heard the truth and told it to Queen Esther so that she could tell the king. Follow the path beginning with the ear, around the crown and finish at the lips.

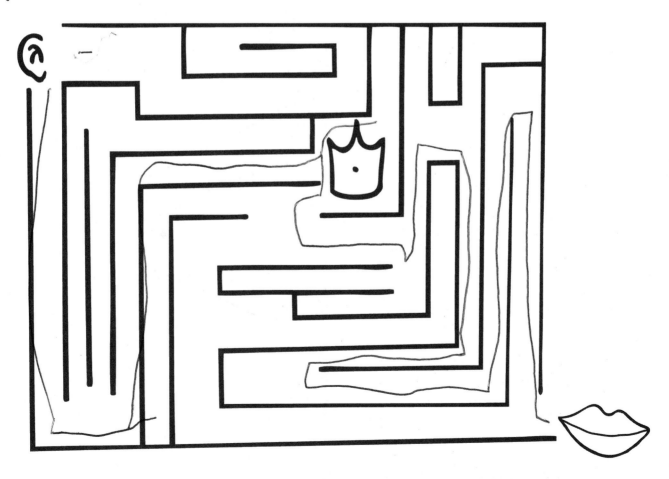

A Dangerous Decree

memory verse
....
All the royal officials at the king's gate knelt down and paid honor to Haman...
but Mordecai would not kneel down or pay him honor. ~Esther 3:2

Mordecai Refuses to Bow
Down to Haman (Esther 3:1–6)

Haman was the highest official to King Xerxes. All the royal officials were supposed to bow down and honor Haman. Mordecai refused because he was a Jew and worshipped only God. This made Haman mad. He asked the king for a decree to destroy the Jews for not bowing down to him. King Xerxes granted the decree. Neither Haman nor the king knew that Queen Esther was a Jew.

What to Do

✳ What is a decree? Follow the spaces and substitute the letter for the number in each one. The number will correspond to the letter's place in the alphabet. For example, 1=A, 2=B and so on. Move counter clockwise from "Start."

__ __   __ __ __ __ __

__ __ __ __ __ __

__ __ __ __ __

__ __ __   __ __ __ __ __

__ __   __ __ __ __   __ __ __.

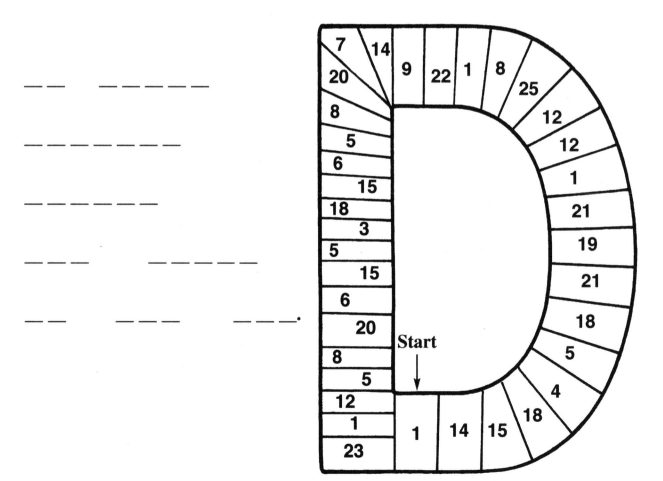

128

Job Obeys No Matter What

memory verse

In all this, Job did not sin. ~Job 1:22

God is With Us (Job 1)

Job obeyed God even when bad things happened. Lots of bad things happened to Job. A storm destroyed his house and all his children died. He got very sick. Lots of other bad things happened too. But Job still trusted God. God took care of Job because he obeyed Him. God made Job well and gave him more children. God is with us even when bad things happen.

What to Do

✱ These pictures tell about Job. But they are all mixed up. Can you number them in the correct order? The first one is done for you.

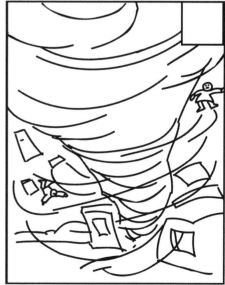

Job's Friends Try to Make Him Disobey

memory verse

How long will you torment me and crush me with words? ~Job 19:2

Refusing to Disobey (Job 2-37)

Job's wife and three friends tried to get him to curse God and give up. But Job refused to disobey God. What could you say if a friend tried to make you disobey God?

What to Do

* Help Job find the altar.

Praying to God

Prayer (Psalm 4:3)

Prayer is talking to God. We can talk to God any time. We can talk to God anywhere and we can talk to God about anything.

God wants us to talk to Him all the time. Sometimes it is hard to pray because there are many people around or because it is noisy. God will hear your prayer anyway.

When you pray, you can tell God "thank You" for the good things He does for you. One good time to say "thank You" to God is before you eat.

What to Do

✱ Follow the dots to see what the boy is doing before he eats his lunch. Sometimes people might laugh at you for praying, but Jesus is with you to help you do what He wants you to do.

God Uses Children

memory verse
. . . .
I knew you before you were born. ~Jeremiah 1:5

A Special Plan (Jeremiah 1:1-6)

God called Jeremiah to be a prophet while Josiah was king. He must have been young because he complained to the Lord, "I am only a child." God told Jeremiah that He knew him before he was born. God had a special job for Jeremiah. He would call the people of Israel to repent of their sins. God knew you before you were born, too. He has a special plan for you.

What to Do

✴ Start with the large D at the arrow and, moving clockwise, write every other letter on the lines until you have gone around the circle two times. You will spell the names of five boys that God called at a young age.

1. D _ _ _ _ _

2. J _ _ _ _ _

3. S _ _ _ _ _ _

4. M _ _ _ _ _

5. J _ _ _ _ _ _

God Made Me
for a Special Purpose

memory verse
. . . .
Your love, Lord, endures forever. ~Psalm 138:8

Plans for Jeremiah (Jeremiah 1:1-6)

God called Jeremiah to be a prophet to His people. Jeremiah was reluctant because he was young. God told Jeremiah that He had plans for Jeremiah before he was even born. God has special plans for all of us.

What to Do

✱ What did Jeremiah tell God? To find out cross out all of the small letters.

Ib AdM

yOwqNzLuoY

wA

fCkmHpIanLzvDj

___ ____ _____

___ _____

133

The King's Food

memory verse

Whatever you do, do it all for the glory of God. ~1 Corinthians 10:31

Good Health (Daniel 1:3-10)

Daniel and his friends were captured by the Babylonians. The king of Babylon wanted them to work for him. The king wanted them to eat his rich food and drink his wine. But Daniel said, "No! This would not please our God." So Daniel and his friends ate vegetables and drank water. At the end of ten days they were stronger than anyone who ate the king's food. The king saw this and was pleased. God was pleased, too. God gave Daniel and his friends wisdom to help the king. We should also take good care of our bodies so we can be strong to do what God commands.

What to Do

✳ Should Daniel eat snacks or good food if he wants to be strong for God? Help him find the way to the best food.

134

Far From Home

memory verse
. . . .
Whoever trusts in the Lord is kept safe. ~Proverbs 29:25

Worship Only God (Daniel 3 and 6)

Soldiers from Babylon tore down Jerusalem and took many of the people as slaves. Among those taken were Daniel and his friends, Shadrach, Meshach and Abednego. In Babylon, these boys were asked to bow down to idols. They refused to obey! Even when the king threw Daniel in a den of lions he would not bow down. God took care of Daniel. When the king threw Shadrach, Meshach and Abednego into a fiery furnace they would not bow down to idols either. God kept them safe, too. God protects those who follow Him. Below are some examples of things we might make idols of and worship instead of God. Worshipping these things is not good for us.

What to Do

✳ Daniel and his friends would not bow down to idols. Circle the example you should follow and cross out the others.

Who's the King?

Handwriting on the Wall (Daniel 5)

There are many bad kings in the Bible. One in particular spent too much time having parties and large dinners. He thought that because his kingdom had high walls and large gates, his enemies couldn't get to him. During one party, he drank a toast to false gods. Suddenly, a hand appeared and wrote on a wall. God sent the hand to tell the evil king that his enemies were going to conquer his kingdom. The king was killed that very night!

What to Do

✶ To find out the name of the bad king, solve the two-part puzzle. First, use the clues to fill in the blanks next to the animal pictures. Then place the numbered letters in the matching numbered blanks at the bottom to spell the name of the king.

An animal that says, "Quack."

___ ___ ___ ___
1   2   3   4

An animal with stripes.

___ ___ ___ ___ ___
5   6   7   8   9

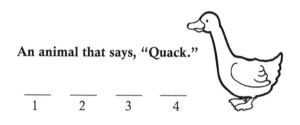

An animal with a trunk.

___ ___ ___ ___ ___ ___ ___ ___
10 11 12 13 14 15 16 17

An animal that roars.

___ ___ ___ ___
18 19 20 21

What a hen lays.

___ ___ ___
22 23 24

A little animal that gives off a bad smell.

___ ___ ___ ___ ___
25 26 27 28 29

___ ___ ___ ___   ___ ___ ___ ___ ___ ___ ___ ___ ___
4   19 28 23   7   22 11 25 14 9   5   5   9   8

Daniel in the Lions' Den

memory verse

Three times a day he got down on his knees and prayed. ~Daniel 6:10

God Saves Daniel (Daniel 6)

Each day Daniel prayed to God. Some bad men did not like Daniel. They made a rule. They said that the people could only pray to the king. That didn't keep Daniel from praying to God! Then the bad men caught Daniel praying. They threw him into a den of hungry lions. But God saved Daniel!

What to Do

✱ Daniel spent the night in the lions' den. Can you tell which lion is different? Color it, then color the rest of the picture.

A Den Full of Lions

memory verse

He whose walk is blameless is kept safe. ~Proverbs 28:18

God Protects Daniel (Daniel 6)

The Bible tells a story about a man named Daniel who loved God very much. Every day Daniel prayed to God. There were some angry men who didn't love God and hated Daniel. They forced the king to make a bad rule. The rule said that if anyone prayed to God, they must be thrown into a den of hungry lions. The king liked Daniel and didn't know that this rule would hurt Daniel. Do you think Daniel stopped praying to God? No, he did not. So when the men caught him, they threw Daniel in the lions' den. But God did not let the lions hurt Daniel. The king was happy that God helped his friend. Aren't you happy, too?

What to Do

✳ There are four lions hiding in this den. Can you find them?

Disobedience Smells Fishy

memory verse

Jonah ran away from the Lord. . ~Jonah 1:3

Swallowed and Saved (Jonah 1)

God told Jonah to go to Nineveh. But Jonah hopped on a boat and went the other way. God was not pleased. He sent a storm. The sailors thought Jonah caused the storm so they threw him overboard. God saved Jonah by sending a big fish to swallow him. God doesn't like when we disobey Him, but He will always forgive and save us when we ask.

What to Do

* Connect the dots to see where Jonah landed when he disobeyed God.

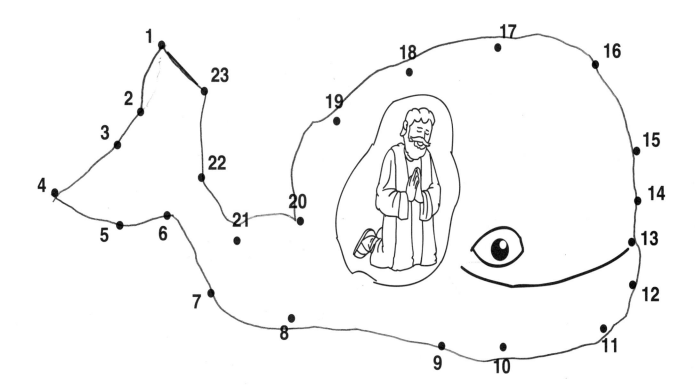

A Big Fish

Jonah Escapes (Jonah 1:17-2:1, 2:10)

The Lord provided a great fish to swallow Jonah, and Jonah was inside the fish three days and three nights. From inside the fish Jonah prayed to the Lord his God . . . And the Lord commanded the fish, and it vomited Jonah onto dry land.

What to Do

✻ Jonah, a prophet of God, did not want to do what God had asked him. God gave him time to think about it — in the belly of a big fish! Once Jonah had asked for God's forgiveness, the fish spat him back out onto the land. Use the Scripture to find clues to fill in the crossword puzzle.

Down
1. Water creature with fins and gills
2. Gave
3. Solid part of the earth's surface
4. God
6. The inner part
9. After dawn (plural)
11. On top of
12. Ordered

Across
2. Talked with God
5. Consume
7. Was swallowed by a whale
8. After dusk (plural)
10. The Almighty Father
13. Ejected from the stomach by mouth
14. Opposite of wet
15. Extremely large
16. 2+1

Back on the Road to Nineveh

memory verse

Jonah obeyed the word of the Lord and went to Nineveh. ~Jonah 3:3

Now to Ninevah! (Jonah 2; 3:1-3)

Jonah sat inside the belly of the big fish. He prayed a lot. He thought about how he had disobeyed God. After three days the fish spat Jonah out onto the beach. Jonah had learned his lesson. He obeyed God and headed for Nineveh. Sometimes God has to teach us a lesson when we disobey Him.

What to Do

✱ Jonah doesn't want to go the wrong way again. Can you help him find his way to Nineveh?

Teaching Others to Obey

memory verse
He will teach us his ways ~Micah 4:2

The People Listen to Jonah (Jonah 3:4-10)

Jonah told the people of Nineveh that God was not happy with them. The people there worshiped idols instead of God. They listened to Jonah. They changed and worshiped God instead. We should always remember to worship the one, true God.

What to Do

✳ Nineveh was a crowded city. Jonah told the people to change their ways. Can you find Jonah in the crowd? Color him, then color the rest of the picture.

Where is Jonah?

Fleeing to Egypt

memory verse

. . . .
I will counsel you and watch over you. ~Psalm 32:8

A Star in the Sky (Matthew 2)

After Jesus was born there were wise men who came from far away to see Him. They followed a star in the sky. It led the wise men to Jerusalem. There they asked King Herod where the baby was. Herod told them to go to Bethlehem, because he knew the prophets had said that was where the Savior would be born. The wise men found Jesus with Joseph and Mary in Bethlehem. They were so happy to see the baby! They brought Him wonderful gifts. God warned the wise men in a dream not to tell Herod. Then God warned Joseph to take baby Jesus to Egypt, because King Herod wanted to kill the boy. They left during the night and did not return until Herod was long dead.

What to Do

✳ Study this picture for one minute. Turn the page over and see how many things you can remember from the picture. Tell a friend.

Mary and Joseph Obey the Angel

memory verse

....

Joseph did what the angel of the Lord had commanded him. ~Matthew 1:24

God Protects Us (Matthew 1:18–2:23)

Several times God sent an angel to tell Joseph what to do for Mary and baby Jesus. God protects us when we obey Him.

What to Do

✶ Compare the pictures from the first column to those in the second column. What is missing from each picture in the second column? Draw the missing parts to each picture.

Warning Code

memory verse

An angel of the Lord appeared to Joseph in a dream. "Get up," he said, "take the child and his mother and escape to Egypt. Stay there until I tell you."

~Matthew 2:13

Joseph, Mary and Jesus Flee to Egypt

(Matthew 2:13-20)

King Herod instructed the wise men to tell him where he could find the king of the Jews. King Herod was afraid the new king would get rid of him, so he ordered that all boys ages 2 and under be killed. The wise men followed the star to Bethlehem and found Jesus. After they left, an angel warned Joseph to take his family and flee to Egypt. Joseph took Mary and Jesus to Egypt.

What to Do

✱ Use the NATO Phonetic Alphabet code below to find out what warning Joseph received.

NATO Phonetic Alphabet

Echo	**Foxtrot**	**Golf**	**Lima**
E	F	G	L

Oscar	**Papa**	**Tango**	**Yankee**
O	P	T	Y

F L e e
Foxtrot **Lima** **Echo** **Echo**

T O e G Y P T
Tango **Oscar** **Echo** **Golf** **Yankee** **Papa** **Tango**

The Long Journey Maze

memory verse
An angel of the Lord appeared to Joseph in a dream. "Get up," he said, "take the child and his mother and escape to Egypt." ~Matthew 2:13

Protecting Jesus (Matthew 2:13-23)

One night an angel appeared to Joseph in a dream and warned him, "Herod wants to kill the young child. Get up and take Him and His mother away." Joseph obeyed at once, taking the family on a long journey to another country. Herod killed all the boys in Bethlehem who were under the age of two, but Jesus was safe.

What to Do

✶ Where did Joseph take Mary and Jesus? You will find the answer as you work the maze. Joseph kept his family in that country until Herod was dead and it was safe to return to their own land. Finish the maze to discover the name of this town.

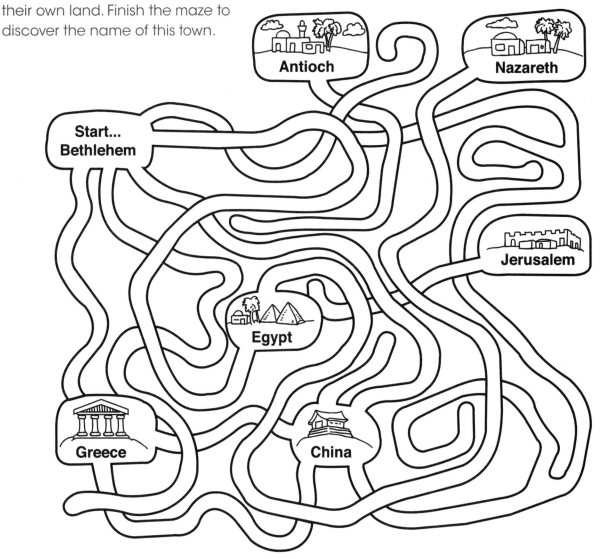

A Secret Message

A Faithful Cousin (Matthew 3:1-12)

John the Baptist was Jesus' cousin. He preached forgiveness to people. "Are you the Christ who has come to save us?" some of them asked. John the Baptist said, "I am not. The Christ is much greater than I. I am not worthy to untie His sandals. I am just here to tell you that the One Who is coming will cause your darkness to be light."

John obeyed Jesus when He asked him to do something for Him.

What to Do

✱ Do the puzzle below to find out what Jesus asked John to do. Write the answer for each item described, then read down the first column to solve the puzzle. Write the letters of the first column in the blanks at the bottom of the page.

Holds pickles, jelly and baby food

Opposite of closed

What you wear on your head to keep warm

What birds lay their eggs in

A newborn

One a day keeps the doctor away

What you cook in

A toy that spins

What cools a drink

Where a collection of wild animals is kept

Opposite of West

Not up

Another name for Christ

Not difficult

A large boat

Opposite of over

What our eyes do

___ ___ ___ ___   ___ ___ ___ ___ ___   ___ ___ ___ ___

New Life Puzzle

memory verse

And a voice came from heaven: "You are my Son, whom I love; with you I am well pleased." ~Luke 3:22

John the Baptist
with Jesus (Matthew 3:7-17; Luke 3:4-22)

John baptized those who showed everyone that they wanted to follow God. To baptize them, John dipped them under the water of the Jordan River. One day, Jesus asked John to baptize Him. John knew Jesus was God's Son. John asked, "Why do You want me to baptize You? I need to be baptized by You." Jesus said it was God's will. As John was bringing Jesus out of the water, the Holy Spirit came down in the form of a dove and God's voice said, "You are my Son, whom I love; with you I am well pleased."

What to Do

✱ When we ask Jesus to forgive our sins, He also forgets our sins. The people who asked John to baptize them were telling others they had decided to stop making wrong choices and were ready to live brand-new lives.

Mark out all the boxes below that contain the letters Q, X or Z. Write the letter that remains in each column in the box directly below that column. The answer will be the Bible hero who said "I baptize you with water."

Q	Z	Z	Q	T	Z	Z	Q	Q	X	Q	Q	X	Q
J	Q	Q	Z	Q	Z	Q	Z	Z	Q	Q	Z	Q	Z
Q	Q	Q	Q	Q	X	Q	X	Q	P	Q	Q	Q	Q
X	X	X	X	Q	Q	Q	X	Q	Q	X	Q	X	T
X	Q	Q	Q	X	Q	X	Q	X	Q	X	Q	X	Q
X	O	Q	Q	X	X	E	Q	X	Q	X	X	Q	Q
X	X	X	N	X	X	Q	X	Q	X	Q	Q	S	Q
Q	X	Q	X	X	X	X	B	Q	X	Q	X	X	X
Q	X	H	Q	Q	Q	X	X	X	Q	X	Q	X	X
X	Q	X	Q	X	X	Q	X	Q	X	T	X	Q	X
X	X	X	X	X	X	Q	Q	Q	Q	Q	I	Q	Q
X	Q	Q	Q	X	H	X	Q	A	Q	X	Q	Q	X
Q	Q	Q	X	X	X	Q	Q	Q	X	X	X	Q	X

Run from Satan

memory verse
. . . .
Flee the evil desires of youth. ~2 Timothy 2:22

Which Way? (Matthew 4:1-17)

Jesus went to the wilderness to pray. Satan knew He was tired and hungry. Jesus ran from Satan and obeyed God. We should stay away from evil and follow God, too.

What to Do

✳ Draw a path from Jesus to the open end where He can escape from Satan.

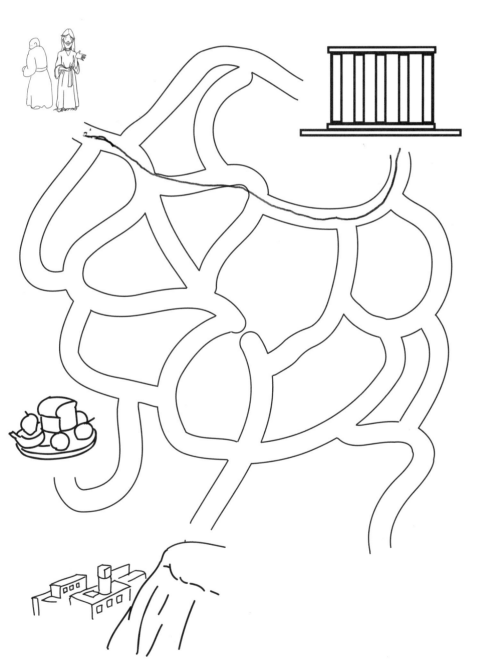

Fisherman of Men

I will make you fishers of men. ~Matthew 4:19

A Full Catch (Matthew 4:18-20)

Peter was a fisherman. He worked hard. One day Jesus came by. He told Peter, "I will make you a fisherman of men. Leave your net and follow Me." Jesus meant that Peter would teach people to know God. Peter obeyed and followed Jesus. Peter left his net full of fish and followed Jesus. God wants us to follow Him.

What to Do

✳ Can you count the fish in the net?
Color all of the fish.
What did Peter learn to catch?

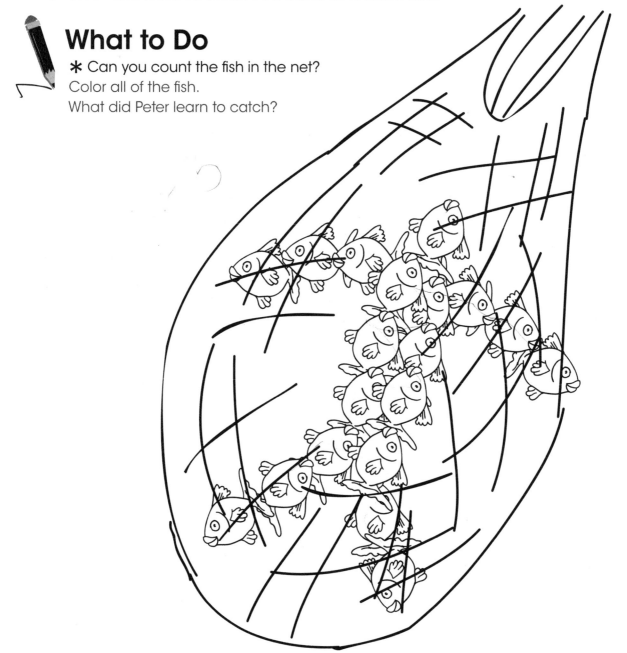

The Beatitudes

Blessed are the Meek (Matthew 5:3-10)

"Blessed are the poor in spirit, for theirs is the kingdom of heaven. Blessed are those who mourn, for they will be comforted. Blessed are the meek, for they will inherit the earth. Blessed are those who hunger and thirst for righteousness, for they will be filled. Blessed are the merciful, for they will be shown mercy. Blessed are the pure in heart, for they will see God. Blessed are the peacemakers, for they will be called sons of God. Blessed are those who are persecuted because of righteousness, for theirs is the kingdom of heaven."

What to Do

✱ Large crowds followed Jesus to hear His teachings. At what has become known as "The Sermon on the Mount," Jesus taught the Beatitudes. Sometimes the Beatitudes are described as the "Be-Attitudes" because they tell about good ways to act. Read the Scripture that tells of each Beatitude as you look for clues to fill in the crossword puzzle.

Down
2. Those who show kindness
3. Given prosperity or happiness
4. Suffering because of belief
5. Free from moral fault or guilt
7. Come into possession of
8. Grieve
10. Desire for liquids
13. Having little money
16. Named
17. The planet we live on
19. Male offspring

Across
1. Country ruled by a king
6. Those who make peace
9. Uprightness
11. Great Creator
12. Desire for food
14. The soul
15. Kindness
16. Soothed
18. Full
20. Humble
21. God's home

Jesus Talks to the People

memory verse
· ·
Rejoice and be glad. ~Matthew 5:12

Jesus on the Mountain Top (Matthew 5-7; Luke 6:17-49)

One day Jesus went high up on a mountain. Many people followed Him there. They wanted to listen to Him teach. Jesus loved telling the people about God. Jesus told the people, "Blessed are you." He told them that they would be happy and blessed if they obeyed and loved God. He told them that if they were sad, God would comfort them. Jesus said that they must be like Him. Do you want to be like Jesus?

What to Do

✱ Color this picture of Jesus talking to people using the color key.

Color the △ blue.   Color the ○ green.   Color the □ red.

Color the ◆ yellow.   Color the ✱ brown.

Let Your Light Shine

Praise Your Father in Heaven (Matthew 5:14-16)

"You are the light of the world. A city on a hill cannot be hidden. Neither do people light a lamp and put it under a bowl. Instead they put it on its stand, and it gives light to everyone in the house. In the same way, let your light shine before men, that they may see your good deeds and praise your Father in heaven."

What to Do

✳ Jesus often taught using parables, or stories. This parable teaches that we should let our light shine to the world so others will know we love Jesus. Use the Scripture to find clues to fill in the crossword puzzle.

Down
1. Male parent
3. All people
4. Acts
6. Many persons
7. Building in which you live
9. A platform on which something is placed
11. Land form smaller than a mountain
12. 2nd person pronoun
16. More than one adult male

Across
2. To glorify
5. Reflect light
7. Put out of sight
8. Not bad
10. Brightness we get from the sun
11. Where God lives
13. A curved vessel for holding food or liquids
14. Universe
15. Electric device for producing light

Where Do We Pray?

memory verse
The Lord...hears the prayer of the righteous. ~Proverbs 15:29

A Quiet Place (Matthew 6:5-8)

Jesus taught us where and how we should pray or talk to God. He told us that we can talk to God anywhere and at anytime. But we must not pray so that others will hear us and think we are special because of our prayers. We should find a quiet place to pray to God. Where do you think would be a good place to pray to God?

What to Do

✱ In this room there are five boys quietly praying to God. Can you find them?

Be Clean!

Jesus Cures a Leper (Matthew 8:1-3)

When he came down from the mountainside, large crowds followed him. A man with leprosy came and knelt before him and said, "Lord, if you are willing, you can make me clean."

Jesus reached out his hand and touched the man. "I am willing," he said. "Be clean!" Immediately he was cured of his leprosy.

What to Do

✱ Jesus performed many miracles during His ministry. One involved a man who had leprosy. Use the Scripture to find clues to fill in the crossword puzzle.

Down
1. Big
2. Did come
6. Part of large natural elevation of the earth's surface
7. A disease of sores on the body
8. Part of the body below the wrist
9. Many people
10. Did kneel
12. Made physical contact

Across
1. Master
3. Made well
4. Human adult male
5. Right now
11. From higher to lower
13. Came after
14. Extended the hand
15. Free from impurities
16. Having the intention
17. God's Son

Matthew Obeys Jesus

memory verse

Matthew got up and followed him.   ~Matthew 9:9

Matthew Follows Jesus (Matthew 9:9-10)

One day Jesus walked by a man named Matthew sitting in a tax collector's booth. Jesus told Matthew, "Come follow Me." Matthew obeyed Jesus. He left his booth and all his money to follow Jesus.

What to Do

✱ Can you find 4 things wrong with this picture? Circle them.

TAXES
COLLECTED HERE

Jairus' Daughter Brought to Life

memory verse
. . . .
The Mighty One has done great things for me — holy is his name ~Luke 1:49

Jesus Saves
a Little Girl (Matthew 9:18-26; Mark 5:22-43; Luke 8:41-56)

Jairus ran up to Jesus. "Please come to my house. My little girl is dying," Jairus pleaded. Jesus went with Jairus, but it was too late. People were crying. Jairus' daughter had died. Jesus made all the people go away. He told the little girl, "Wake up!" What do you think the little girl did? Jairus' daughter got up. She was alive again! Can you make a dead person come alive? No, only Jesus, God's Son, can do that. Do you think that Jairus was happy? Jesus can do anything!

What to Do

✱ Jairus daughter had died, but Jesus brought her back to life. Look at these pictures. They tell the story. Number the pictures in the order that they happened.

Nothing is Impossible

 memory verse

Nothing will be impossible for you. ~Matthew 17:21

Have Faith (Matthew 17:19-21)

The apostles were frustrated that they could not help a sick boy. Jesus told them it was because they did not have enough faith. He told them that it takes just a little bit of faith to do big things. If they would trust and believe, He said, they could do anything.

What to Do

✱ Jesus said a little faith can do big things.
Circle the things in each row that are little.

Blessed Are the Merciful

memory verse

Forgive your brother from the heart. ~Matthew 18:35

Showing Mercy (Matthew 18:21-35)

Jesus told His disciples a story to teach them how they should forgive anyone who hurts them. He said a man owed the king a lot of money. The king wanted the man to pay the debt. The man had no money. So the king ordered that the man sell his wife and children to pay the debt. But the man pleaded with the king to cancel the debt. The king felt sorry for the man and let him go. Do you think the man was thankful? He went out and found someone who owed him money. He grabbed him by the neck and said, "Pay me what you owe me!" The other servant asked for time to pay it back. But the man had him thrown in jail. What do you think the king did when he found this out? He was very angry and threw the first man in jail. "I forgave your debt!" he said. "Why didn't you forgive the debt of the other servant?" Jesus told His disciples that God will not forgive us and give us mercy if we don't show mercy to others.

What to Do

✳ These pictures tell the story of the unmerciful servant. They are all mixed up. Number them in the correct order.

Let the Little Children Come

memory verse
....
Let the little children come to me. ~Matthew 19:14

Lots of Kids (Matthew 19:13-15; Mark 10:13-16)

Sometimes it may seem like adults are too busy to talk or play with you. Jesus was never too tired to spend time with children. One day Jesus was busy teaching a group of people. Some mothers came to Jesus. They wanted Him to hold and touch their children. The disciples stopped them, saying, "Jesus is too tired and busy. Go away." Jesus heard them and stopped them. "Let the little children come to me," He said. Jesus placed them on His lap. He gave them all a big hug and blessed them. Jesus always has time for everyone.

What to Do

✳ Mothers brought their children to Jesus. Can you find two sets of twins in this picture?

A Story About Two Sons

memory verse
....
Repent and believe ~Matthew 21:32

Two Different Sons (Matthew 21:28-32)

Jesus told a story about a man who had two sons. He went to the first son and said, "Son, please work in the vineyard." The son answered, "No, I don't feel like it today." But the son changed his mind and went later. Then the father went to his second son and asked the same thing. The son said, "Sure, I will go." But this son never went. Jesus asked those listening, "Which son did what his father wanted?" Which son do you think was obedient?

What to Do

✱ The two sons in the story acted very differently from one another. Look at each row of pictures. Which object is different from the others?

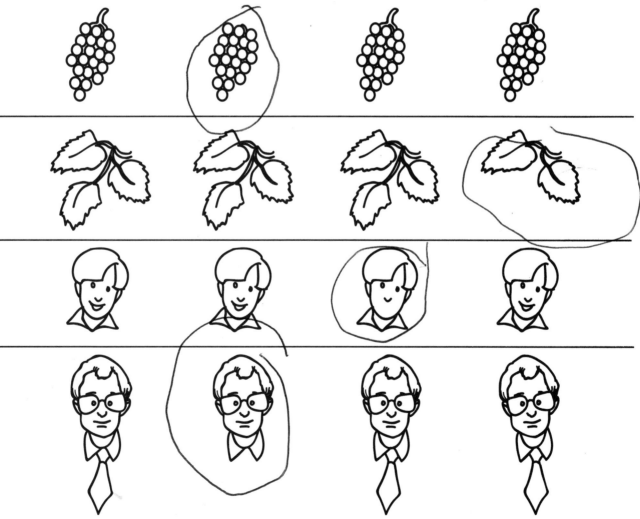

A Friend Shares His Tomb

memory verse
. . . .
Joseph took the body, wrapped it in a clean linen cloth, and placed it
in his own new tomb.   ~Matthew 27:59-60

Joseph Cares for Jesus (Matthew 27:57-61)

A man named Joseph was a member of the group that killed Jesus. But Joseph had
become Jesus' disciple. After Jesus died, Joseph asked Pilate for the body. Pilate agreed,
so Joseph took the body and wrapped it in clean cloth. Then he placed it in a cave. (In
Bible times, dead bodies were placed in caves instead of buried underground.) It was
Joseph's own burial tomb. He had it prepared for when he died. But Joseph loved Jesus.
He wanted Jesus to be buried in a clean, new place. Then a big stone was rolled over
the front of the cave. Several women who loved Jesus watched as Jesus' body was laid
in the tomb. It was almost time for the Sabbath. Everyone went home to rest and to hurt
over the loss of Jesus. What a sad day!

What to Do

✳ Look at these pictures. They tell the story of Jesus' burial. Number the pictures in
the correct order.

The First Easter

He Has Risen (Matthew 28:5-7)

The angel said to the women, "Do not be afraid, for I know that you are looking for Jesus, who was crucified. He is not here; he has risen, just as he said. Come and see the place where he lay. Then go quickly and tell his disciples: 'He has risen from the dead and is going ahead of you into Galilee. There you will see him.' Now I have told you."

What to Do

✱ After Jesus was betrayed, He was crucified on the cross and died. But He didn't stay in the grave. He rose again and is alive today. We celebrate His resurrection at Easter. The Scripture has clues that will help you fill in the crossword puzzle.

Down
1. Did tell
2. God's messenger
3. Not alive
6. Did say
7. Killed by nailing to a cross
8. At this place
11. Next in time, order
12. Place on a surface
14. At this moment
18. Perceive with the eye
20. From the outside
21. A portion of space

Across
4. Using the eyes
5. God's Son
9. Scared
10. In front
11. To express with words
13. More than one woman
15. Ascended
16. Be aware of
17. Fast
19. Followers
22. Beginning at
23. Approach

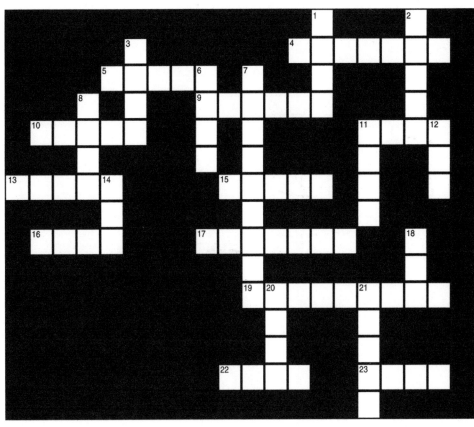

A Man Comes Through the Roof

memory verse

Get up, take your mat and walk. ~Mark 2:9

Bible Story (Mark 2:1-12)

One day Jesus was teaching in a house. The house was so full of people there was no more room. Some men brought their friend who was sick. They knew that Jesus could make him well. But they could not get their friend into the house. Do you know what they did? They made a hole in the roof and lowered their friend down to Jesus. "Please help our friend. He cannot walk," the men told Jesus. Jesus was happy to see how much the men cared for their sick friend. "Get up," said Jesus. "Take your mat and go home." The man was so happy. His friends were happy, too. Do you think the man went back out through the roof?

What to Do

✻ Look at the two pictures on this page. Cover the second one as you look at the first one. Now cover the first one. How many things are missing from the second picture that were in the first one?

Jesus Prepares a Big Lunch

memory verse

And my God will meet all your needs according to his glorious riches in Christ Jesus. ~Philippians 4:19

A Little Boy Shares His Food (Mark 6:30-44)

Has your mom ever fixed lunch or dinner for lots of people? Jesus did. One day Jesus was speaking to a big crowd. There were 5,000 people. (Your mom never fed that many!) It was late and the crowd became hungry. A little boy had brought his lunch. But it was not enough to feed 5,000! All he had were two small fish and five loaves of bread. But Jesus asked him to share it anyway. The boy was happy to give his food to Jesus. Jesus prayed and began breaking the bread and fish. He passed it to the people. Jesus kept breaking and breaking and breaking the food. Soon everyone had enough to eat. When Jesus' helpers picked up the leftovers there were 12 baskets full of bread and fish. Now that was a big lunch!

What to Do

✳ Hidden in this picture are ~~two fish, five loaves of bread and 12 baskets~~. Can you find them?

Find the Hidden Pictures

Jesus Blesses the Children (Mark 10:13-16)

Jesus loves children. When He lived on earth, He was very happy when children came to see Him. He held the children in His arms and He blessed them.

Now that Jesus is in heaven, He still loves children. He loves you and He can be with you all the time. He wants to be your friend if you will ask Him.

What to Do

✽ Look at the picture. Jesus likes trees, flowers, grass and other things, but He loves children. There are five hidden flowers in the picture. Can you find them?

A Rich Young Man

memory verse
. . . .
All things are possible with God. ~Mark 10:27

The Path to Heaven (Mark 10:17-31)

Some things really make Jesus sad. When someone decides not to follow God, Jesus feels really bad. One day a young man ran up to Jesus and asked, "What must I do to go to heaven?" Jesus said, "Keep all the commandments. Honor your mother and father, do not steal, do not tell lies." The man smiled and said, "I've kept all the commandments since I was a little boy." He thought for sure he would go to heaven. Then Jesus said, "Sell everything you have and give it to the poor. Then you will have riches in heaven." The man was sad. He was very rich. He could not do this, so he walked away from Jesus. Jesus said that it is very hard for a rich man to get to heaven. But we can be saved because all things are possible for God.

What to Do

✳ The young man wanted to go to heaven. See if you can help him get there. What did he choose?

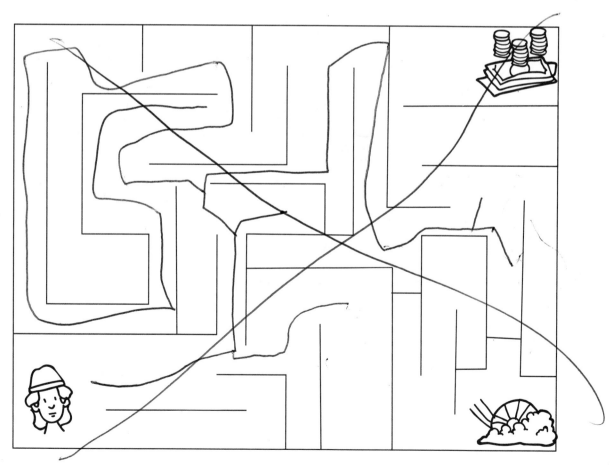

The Fig Tree

Jesus Uses the Fig Tree to Teach (Mark 13:28-29)

"Now learn this lesson from the fig tree: As soon as its twigs get tender and its leaves come out, you know that summer is near. Even so, when you see these things happening, you know that it is near, right at the door."

What to Do

✳ Jesus wants His followers to be prepared for His return because we don't know when it will be. However, Jesus said there would be signs of His return. In this passage, He compares the signs to a fig tree. Use the Scripture to find clues to fill in the crossword puzzle.

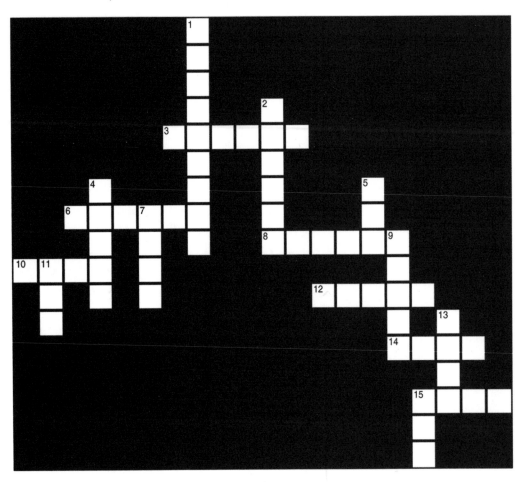

Down
1. Taking place
2. Green "plants" attached to stems on trees
4. Gain knowledge or understanding
5. Perceive with the eye
7. In the near future
9. Opposite of left
11. Away from inside
13. Close
15. Sweet fruit that grows on trees

Across
3. Soft
6. Something learned
8. Between spring and fall
10. Movable panel used to close entranceway
12. Small branches
14. Plant that has a trunk
15. Because of

An Empty Tomb

memory verse
They saw that the stone...had been rolled away. ~Mark 16:4

Jesus is Alive! (Mark 16:1-11)

The Sabbath was over. Some women went to Jesus' tomb very early in the morning. They planned to put spices on His body. They said, "Who will help us roll the stone?" When they got to the tomb the stone was already rolled away. Suddenly an angel appeared. "Don't be afraid!" he said. "Jesus has risen! See, His body is gone." The women were so excited. The angel told them to run and tell the other disciples that Jesus is alive! Then Jesus appeared to Mary, one of the women. She was so happy to see Jesus! She ran and told everyone, "Jesus is alive!" Wouldn't that be wonderful news to share with your friends?

What to Do

✱ Read the sentences below. There are missing words. Look at the word box. Which words would you choose? Write the words on the lines.

The women asked each other, "Who will help us roll the _____?"

"Don't be _____!"
said the angel.

"Jesus is_____!"

died
afraid
door
stone
silly
alive

Special Cousins

memory verse
. . . .
For nothing is impossible with God. ~Luke 1:37

Preparing for Jesus (Luke 1)

When God told Mary that she would give birth to the Savior, she was afraid. It seemed impossible since she was not married. But God Himself would be the Father of this child. God understood that Mary would need to be comforted at a time like this, so He sent her to spend time with her Aunt Elizabeth. Elizabeth was going to have a special baby, too. Jesus and John, Elizabeth's son, probably played together as boys. When he got older, John prepared the way for Jesus' coming.

What to Do

✱ Draw a line between the boys who could play or work together.

Let Your Fingers Do the Talking

memory verse

And now you will be silent and not able to speak until the day this happens.

~Luke 1:20

Zechariah Meets an Angel
at the Temple (Luke 1:5–25)

Zechariah and Elizabeth had been married many years but they had no children. One day, Zechariah went to the temple to do his priestly duties. The angel Gabriel appeared to him and told him that his prayers had been answered, Elizabeth would have a child! Because Zechariah and his wife were very old, he didn't believe the angel. As punishment for not believing this word from God, Gabriel told Zechariah that he would not be able to speak until Elizabeth gave birth. Zechariah could only use his hands to tell people what happened!

There are many ways to communicate with others. You can write out what you want to say, use sign language or try to act out the words. You can know God's written words by reading your Bible.

What to Do

✷ Pretend you cannot talk as you find the words (listed on each side) in the puzzle below and circle them.

Next, try to make sentences using the words you found. Write them in the blank lines at the bottom of the page. Be creative!

A	HIS
ANGEL	WOULD
NOT	AND
TOLD	NOT
AN	HE
DID	SPEAK
BELIEVE	BABY
WIFE	HAVE
ANGEL	THE
COULD	ZECHARIAH

_____

_____

Prepare the Way

memory verse
. . . .
The child grew and became strong in spirit. ~Luke 1:80

His Name Shall Be... (Luke 1:11-21, 57-80)

The angel told Zechariah, "Your wife Elizabeth will bear you a son, and you are to call him John." When the time came, Elizabeth had a son and there was much rejoicing by her neighbors and relatives. On the eighth day they came to name the child, and Elizabeth said his name would be John. But the relatives and friends asked why he would be named John. Shouldn't he be named after his father? They asked Zechariah, who could not speak. He wrote on a tablet: "His name is John." At that moment Zechariah's tongue was set free and he could speak again. When John grew up, he preached to the people about the coming of Jesus.

What to Do

✳ The angel told Zachariah to give the boy a special name. Cross out all the letters that are in the puzzle more than once to find out what it was. *John*

Special News Telegram

memory verse

"I am the Lord's servant," Mary answered. "May your word to me be fulfilled."

~Luke 1:38

God Chooses Mary to be the Mother of Jesus (Luke 1:26–38)

Joseph was engaged to Mary when an angel told Mary some very special news. Out of all the young women for many generations, the angel said Mary would become the mother of the Son of God. She would give birth to a son, he said, and name Him Jesus. At first, Mary was afraid because she was not ready to be a mother. Gabriel, the angel, told her not to be frightened because God would make it happen. Mary trusted God, calling herself the Lord's servant.

What to Do

✷ Use the Morse code below to decode the good news Mary received from Gabriel.

Code

A	D	E	F	G	H	I
•—	—••	•	••—•	——•	••••	••

M	N	O	R	S	T	Y
——	—•	———	•—•	•••	—	—•——

—— •— •—• —•—— •• ••• — •••• •

MARY   IS   THE

—— ——— — •••• •—• — ———

MOTHER   TO

— •••• • ••• ——— —• ——— ••••

THE SON   OF

——• ——— —••

GOD

173

An Angel Tells Good News

memory verse
. . . .
The Lord is with you. ~Luke 1:28

An Angel Appears (Luke 1:26-38)

Mary was a young woman who loved God very much. One night an angel came to visit her. The angel had wonderful news for Mary. God had chosen her to be the mother of His Son. "You will have a baby," said the angel. "He will be God's Son and you will call Him Jesus." "How can this be?" Mary asked. "I am not married." "God will be the baby's Father," the angel answered. "Do you want to be the mother of God's Son?" asked the angel. "Yes," replied Mary. "I will obey God." God was pleased that Mary would be the mother of His Son, Jesus. Mary thanked God for choosing her. Would you like to thank God for sending His Son?

What to Do

✱ Connect the dots in the picture below to see who brought Mary good news. Color the picture.

A Trip to Bethlehem

memory verse

There was no room for them in the inn. ~Luke 2:7

A Place for a King (Luke 2:1-7)

Mary and Joseph lived in a town called Nazareth. One day, before Jesus was born, they had to travel far away to Bethlehem, the town of David. Joseph's family came from Bethlehem. The king had ordered that everyone return to their hometown to be counted. The city was crowded and busy. Joseph and Mary knocked on many doors looking for a place to stay. Mary's baby was ready to be born. But there was no room anywhere. Finally, an innkeeper told them that they could stay in his stable with his animals. Baby Jesus was born in that stable. Mary wrapped Him in strips of cloth and laid Him in a manger, where the animals ate their straw. Do you think that was a good place for a king to be born? It was for the King of kings, God's Son.

What to Do

✱ Look at the pictures below. The second picture has 6 missing parts. Circle the missing parts. Color the pictures.

The Birth of God's Son

memory verse
. . . .
A Savior has been born to you; he is Christ the Lord. ~Luke 2:11

No Room for Jesus (Luke 2:1-7)

Mary and her husband traveled to Bethlehem. Lots of people had gone to the city because the king had said they must to be counted. It came time for Mary's baby to be born. Joseph looked everywhere for a place to spend the night. There was no room anywhere. Finally an innkeeper said they could stay in his stable with his animals. There, Jesus, God's Son, was born. He would be our Savior and take away our sins. Aren't you glad this special baby was born?

What to Do

✳ Help Mary and Joseph find a place to stay.

A Child is Born!

memory verse
Today a Savior has been born. ~Luke 2:11

A Special Night (Luke 2:1-16)

Mary and Joseph took a trip to Bethlehem to pay their taxes. It was a long way. There were no cars then so they had to ride a donkey or walk. It was an especially hard trip because Mary was going to have a baby. They were very tired. When they got to Bethlehem they could not find a place to stay, so they had to stay in a barn. They slept with cows and horses. During the night a very special child was born to Mary, the baby Jesus. Mary wrapped Him in soft cloth and laid Him in a manger, the place from where animals eat hay. God sent angels to tell the shepherds in the fields to go and see the baby Who would be the Savior.

What to Do

✳ How many things can you find wrong in this picture?

Good News!

A Savior Has Been Born (Luke 2:8-12)

And there were shepherds living out in the fields nearby, keeping watch over their flocks at night. An angel of the Lord appeared to them, and the glory of the Lord shone around them, and they were terrified. But the angel said to them, "Do not be afraid. I bring you good news of great joy that will be for all the people. Today in the town of David a Savior has been born to you; he is Christ the Lord. This will be a sign to you: You will find a baby wrapped in cloths and lying in a manger."

What to Do

✳ The Messiah was born! How would the news be shared? God sent His angels to spread the message. They visited shepherds in the fields. The shepherds knew they had to go see this new child for themselves. Read the Scripture that proclaims this good news to find clues to fill in the crossword puzzle.

Down
2. God
3. Body of persons
4. For-sale house has this in front
5. Feeding trough for horses and cattle
8. Filled with terror
9. Covered
11. One who saves
12. Residing
15. Groups of sheep
17. Past tense of shine
18. Delight; happiness
20. Infant

Across
1. Fabrics
6. Opposite of bad
7. God's messenger
10. Those who tend sheep
13. Filled with fear
14. Became visible
16. Wide open land
19. Close
21. Report of recent events
22. Birthed
23. This day

Angels Tell Shepherds
the Good News

memory verse
. . . .
Glory to God in the highest ~Luke 2:14

A Starry Host (Luke 2:8-20)

There were shepherds taking care of their sheep outside of Bethlehem. God sent an angel to the shepherds. The shepherds were frightened. The angel said, "Do not be afraid. I bring you good news. Today a Savior is born; He is Christ the Lord." The shepherds bowed down before the angel. "Go see for yourself. You will find Him lying in a manger," said the angel. Suddenly the whole sky lit up. Hundreds of angels filled the sky. They sang praises to God. Then the angels left and the sky was dark. "Let's go to Bethlehem," they said. And they ran to find the baby Savior. Would you have liked to have been a shepherd that night?

What to Do

✳ Look at the pictures below. See if you can find a match for each angel, from the right group to the left group. Draw a line between the matching pictures.

Giving Him to God

memory verse
....
Joseph and Mary took him...to present him to the Lord. ~Luke 2:22

Temple Trip (Luke 2:21-39)

Mary and Joseph took Jesus to the temple to be blessed by the priest. As they got closer to the temple, an old man named Simeon came up to them. Simeon was so happy to see Jesus! God had promised the old man that he would see the Savior. Simeon knew immediately that Jesus was the one for whom he had waited. He took the child in his arms and blessed Him. Then an old woman named Anna ran up to Mary and Joseph. She lived in the temple and prayed every day for the coming of the Savior. She gave thanks to God for Jesus. How different the world would be now that He had arrived!

What to Do

✻ Follow Mary and Joseph as they take Jesus to the temple. Who do they meet along the way?

Dot-to-Dot Jesus

memory verse
....
Jesus grew in wisdom and stature. ~Luke 2:52

Jesus is Found at the Temple (Luke 2:40-52)

Joseph, Mary and Jesus walked to Jerusalem to celebrate the Feast of the Passover. Jesus was 12 years old. After the celebration was over, Joseph and Mary and their friends and family started back home. They walked all day, thinking Jesus was with them in the crowd of people. Later when they didn't find Him, Mary and Joseph walked back to Jerusalem to look for Him. They found Jesus in the temple, listening and asking the teachers questions.

What to Do

✱ Color the picture and then connect the dots to find out what Jesus wanted to know about.

Where to Find Jesus

memory verse

"Didn't you know I had to be in my Father's house?" ~Luke 2:49

Jesus Stays at the Temple (Luke 2:40-52)

Jesus parents' realized He was not in their group as they traveled home from Jerusalem. After searching for three days they found Him in the temple courts, listening to the teachers and asking them questions. They were amazed by His understanding of the Bible. He was glad to learn more about God, His Father in heaven. His mother asked Jesus why he had misbehaved by not returning with them. Jesus was surprised. "Didn't you know I had to be in my Father's house?" he asked. At first His parents did not understand, but soon his mother treasured these things as Jesus' wisdom and knowledge of the Bible grew.

What to Do

✱ Color each square that has a number in it. Do not color any squares that have letters in them. Write the letters you find on the blank lines below the square. Unscramble them to find the answer.

6	8	I	7	3	2
B	3	2	5	8	1
9	1	8	4	L	4
3	2	7	3	2	1
1	3	9	B	3	7
7	4	5	8	2	E

 B   B   B   L   e

___ ___ ___ ___ ___

In My Father's House

memory verse

I had to be in my Father's house. ~Luke 2:49

Where is Jesus? (Luke 2:41-50)

When Jesus was 12 years old, He went with Mary and Joseph to Jerusalem to visit the temple. Mary and Joseph returned to Nazareth, but Jesus stayed behind in the temple. Jesus' parents looked for Him. When they could not find Him, they returned to Jerusalem. After three days of searching they found Jesus in the temple. He was talking to the teachers of the Law. The teachers were amazed at Jesus' wisdom and understanding. His parents were upset with Him. Jesus said, "Why were you searching for me? Didn't you know I had to be in my Father's house?"

What to Do

✳ Help Jesus' parents find Him. Follow the maze to find out where Jesus was

Obeying Your Parents

 memory verse
....
[Jesus] was obedient to [his parents]. ~Luke 2:51

Jesus is a Good Son (Luke 2:51)

Jesus obeyed His parents. God was pleased with Jesus. God is pleased when you obey your parents, too.

········▶ **Dad's Helper**

Jesus' earthly father, Joseph, was a carpenter. Jesus probably helped him in his work. Can you find these items in the picture below?

Draw a square around the  .

Draw a line from the ⌐ to the 🪑 .

Color the 🐱 .

Always Obedient

memory verse
. . . .
He was obedient to them. ~Luke 2:51

Jesus Obeyed His Parents (Luke 2:51-52)

Jesus returned with Mary and Joseph to Nazareth. Jesus was a very obedient boy. He helped Joseph work in the carpentry shop. Jesus learned to make chairs and tables. He worked hard and grew strong. Jesus helped Mary, too. He loved His mother very much. Jesus also studied the Law of the Lord. He grew very wise. Jesus made friends and everyone liked Him. God was very pleased.

What to Do

✳ In each row, cross out what does not go with the other two items.

The New Testament

memory verse

In the beginning was the Word, and the Word was with God,
and the Word was God. ~John 1:1

The Word (Luke 4:14-21)

Old Testament people knew that Jesus, God's Son, would someday come into the world.
They wrote about His coming and told people to watch for Him. Years later, after Jesus
did come and was grown up, He went into the synagogue, or church, in His home town.
Jesus stood up and read the Old Testament from a scroll. This writing told of the coming
of a Savior. Jesus was reading about Himself. The New Testament tells about Jesus and
how to obey Him. Jesus is the fulfillment of God's promises in the Old Testament

What to Do

✳ Color black the boxes with X's below. The leftover letters will reveal the person who
was the living Word of God.

X	J	X	X	X
X	X	X	E	X
X	X	X	S	X
U	X	X	X	X
X	X	X	S	X

A High Fever

Jesus Restores Health (Luke 4:38-39)

Jesus left the synagogue and went to the home of Simon. Now Simon's mother-in-law was suffering from a high fever, and they asked Jesus to help her. So he bent over her and rebuked the fever, and it left her. She got up at once and began to wait on them.

What to Do

✳ In today's world, we have high-tech medicine to help us recover from illness. But when Jesus walked the earth, medicine was not as advanced. Jesus offered miraculous healing to people in the name of God. Simon's mother-in-law was one of those Jesus healed. Use the clues in the Scripture to fill in the crossword puzzle.

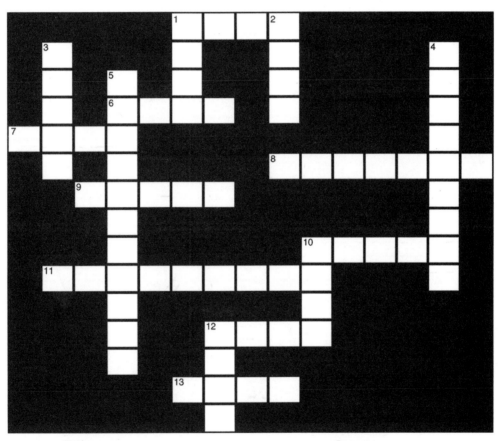

Down
1. The place where one lives
2. Give aid
3. Requested
4. Agony
5. The mother of one's spouse
10. Hunched over
12. Did go

Across
1. Far up
6. Not under
7. Took leave
8. Scolded
9. God's Son
10. Started
11. Place of worship
12. To delay
13. One time

Help the Friends Find Jesus

Jesus Heals a Paralyzed Man (Luke 5:18-26)

Jesus was preaching in a house. Some men carried their friend, who was paralyzed, to the house because they wanted Jesus to heal him. There were so many people listening to Jesus that the men could not get in. So the men made a hole in the roof and lowered their friend down to where Jesus was preaching. Jesus healed the man and he walked home!

What to Do

✳ Help the friends of the sick man find the way to Jesus so their friend can be healed. Then help the man find his way home after Jesus heals him.

A Wise Builder

memory verse
. . . .
If you love me, you will obey what I command. ~John 14:15

Listen to God's Word (Luke 6:46-49)

Jesus told a story to teach His disciples about obeying God. Here is the story He told. There once were two men. Each man planned to build a new house. One man was very wise and chose a good place to build. This wise man built his house on rock. When it rained and the wind blew, his house stood firm. The other man wasn't as smart as the first man. He was in a hurry and built his house on sand. What do you think happened when it rained? His house fell flat. There was no foundation to hold up the house. Jesus said that when we hear God's Word and obey it we are like the wise man. We have a strong foundation. But when we hear God's Word and do not put it into practice we are like the foolish man with the house on sand. Which man do you want to be?

What to Do

✳ It's important to learn how to be a good listener. Name the objects in the top section. Say the names out loud. Listen carefully to the first sound you hear. Circle every object that has the same first sound as ROCK. Do the same in the second box but circle those that have the same first sound as SAND.

A Boy Lives Again

memory verse

God has come to help his people ~Luke 7:16

A Mother and Son (Luke 7:11-17)

Only Jesus can overcome death. One day Jesus saw a crowd carrying a dead person out of town. They were going to bury the young man. He was the only son of a woman. The woman's husband had died and now she would be all alone. Jesus felt sorry for the woman. He told the young man, "Get up!" The boy sat up and began to talk to Jesus. His mother was so happy. Jesus had given her back her son.

What to Do

✱ Connect the mother with her son. Who gave her the boy?

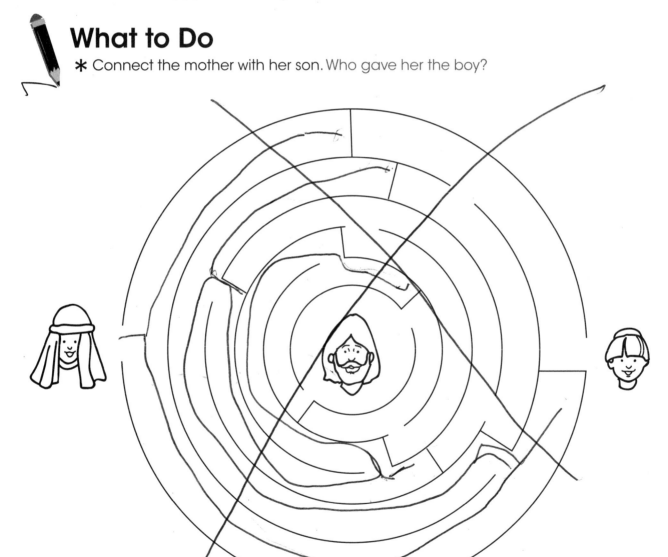

A Wild Man Is Healed

memory verse

Return home and tell how much God has done for you. . ~Luke 8:39

Casting Out Demons (Luke 8:26-39)

Jesus helped a lot of people. He healed them of many illnesses and handicaps. One day, as Jesus was getting out of a boat on a lake, a wild man ran up to Him. The man had lived many years in caves. People had buried dead bodies in the caves. The wild man never wore clothes. Many times the townspeople had locked the wild man in chains. But he always broke loose. He attacked anyone who came near him. Jesus knew that demons, Satan's helpers, had control of the wild man. Jesus ordered, "Leave this man alone!" Then Jesus sent the demons into a herd of pigs eating nearby. The pigs rushed into the lake and drowned. The owners of the pigs were amazed and rushed to tell others in town. The man put clothes on. He sat and talked with Jesus. Aren't you glad that Jesus, the Son of God, is more powerful than Satan and his helpers?

What to Do

✱ Look at the pictures below. See if you can find a match for each picture, from one row to another. Draw a line from the picture on the left to its matching outline on the right.

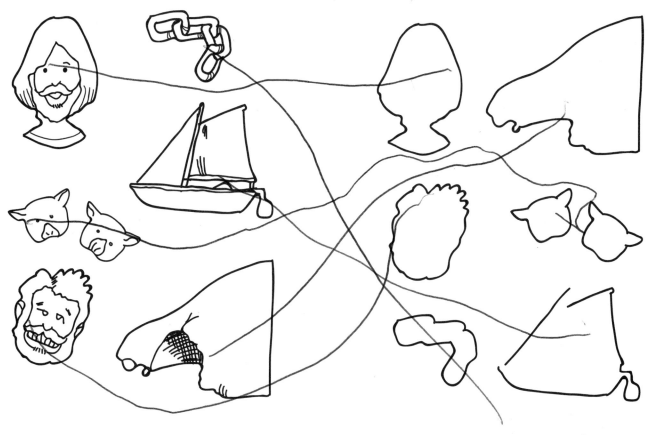

Jesus Wipes Away Our Tears

 memory verse

God will wipe away every tear from their eyes.   ~Revelation 7:17

Jesus Helps (Luke 8:40-56)

Jairus' house was full of people crying over his dead daughter. When Jesus arrived, He sent everyone out of the house. He told them that she was just sleeping. The people laughed, but how happy they were to find out that Jesus had indeed brought this girl back to life. Jesus can help us with any problem we might have.

 ## What to Do

✳ Draw on this face how you think the people felt before Jesus came.

Then draw on this face how you think the people felt once Jesus brought the girl back to life.

Crippled

Jesus Heals a Crippled Woman (Luke 13:11-13)

A woman was there who had been crippled by a spirit for eighteen years. She was bent over and could not straighten up at all. When Jesus saw her, he called her forward and said to her, "Woman, you are set free from your infirmity." Then he put his hands on her, and immediately she straightened up and praised God.

What to Do

✳ Jesus healed many people during His walk on earth. A woman who had been crippled for many years came to see Jesus. Because of her faith, she was healed. Read the Scripture to search for clues to fill in the crossword puzzle.

Down

1. 3 x 6
3. Expressed appreciation
5. Placed
6. Extensions of body below wrists
7. Illness
8. Hunched over
11. The Creator
14. No longer imprisoned
16. Replied
17. Had been able to
18. Put
19. 365 days (plural)

Across

2. From lower to higher
4. Lame or disabled
9. To put in a line
10. God's Son
12. Supernatural being
13. Female adult
15. Out of
20. Above
21. Right now
22. Moved toward the front

The Mustard Seed

Jesus Explains
the Kingdom of God (Luke 13:18-19)

Then Jesus asked, "What is the kingdom of God like? What shall I compare it to? It is like a mustard seed, which a man took and planted in his garden. It grew and became a tree, and the birds of the air perched in its branches."

What to Do

✳ The mustard seed is a very small seed that grows into a very large plant that spreads outward. Jesus compared the kingdom of God to the mustard seed. Just as the mustard plant grows large and spreads, so the Gospel should continue to grow and spread. Red the Scripture for clues to fill in the crossword puzzle.

Down
2. Plot of land used for growing vegetables
3. Yellow condiment
4. Grain of a plant used for sowing
5. God's Son
6. Creator
11. Find likenesses
13. Feathered creatures

Across
1. Place ruled by king
6. Did grow
7. Tall plant with a trunk
8. Questioned
9. Placed in the ground to grow
10. Limbs on a tree
12. Adult male
14. Gaseous mixture surrounding earth
15. Roosted as a bird

A Good Shepherd

memory verse

Rejoice with me; I have found my lost sheep. ~Luke 15:6

A Lost Sheep (Luke 15:1-7)

One day Jesus told His friends about a sheep. The sheep had wandered off from the rest of the flock. It could not find its way back. It was lost! The shepherd counted his sheep and saw that there were only 99, not 100 sheep. He loved all of his sheep and wanted to find the one that was lost. So he left the other sheep and set out to find that one sheep. He looked and looked for his sheep. Finally, he found it! He took it in his arms and returned to the flock. Jesus told this story to teach that we are like sheep. We are far from God. But Jesus is like the shepherd. He loves us and helps us find our way back to God. Aren't you glad Jesus is a Good Shepherd?

What to Do

✱ Find the 6 sheep hidden in the clouds in this picture.

A Lost Coin

memory verse
....
There is rejoicing in the presence of the angels of God
over one sinner who repents. ~Luke 8:10

All of Heaven Rejoices (Luke 15:8-10)

Jesus told stories to teach His followers lessons. Jesus wanted them to understand God.
One story He told was about a woman who had 10 coins. She lost one of the coins. She
looked all over for the coin. She still had nine coins, but wanted the one that was lost.
She swept her house clean until she found the lost coin. Then the woman rejoiced and
told everyone that she had found her coin. Jesus said that is how God feels when one
person repents. All of heaven rejoices.

What to Do

✱ Look at the picture. Draw a circle around all of the silly things in the picture.

196

Party Time Word Search

memory verse
. . . .
The older brother became angry and refused to go in.   ~Luke 15:28

The Oldest Son is Angry (Luke 15:11-30)

A father had two sons. The youngest son wanted his inheritance, so his father gave it to him. The son spent it on foolish things. He returned home to ask for forgiveness. His father gave him a party to celebrate his return home with new wisdom. The older son was angry with his father. He didn't think his younger brother should get a party for his bad choices, so he didn't go. He didn't understand that we should be happy when people ask for forgiveness. It is better to be wise and forgiven than angry and jealous.

What to Do

✱ Find the words from the lesson hidden in the puzzle below. The words might be backward, diagonal, up and down or sideways.

ANGRY	JEALOUS	OLDEST
FATHER	PARTY	YOUNGEST
MUSIC	HARD	WORKED

```
J  D  P  A  R  T  Y  L
R  E  H  T  A  F  O  C
D  K  A  R  K  L  U  I
Y  R  A  L  D  A  N  S
Y  O  A  E  O  R  G  U
A  W  S  H  G  U  E  M
N  T  M  U  S  E  S  C
D  A  N  G  R  Y  T  O
```

The Boy Who Ran Away

 memory verse

This son was lost and is found.   ~Luke 15:24

From Riches to Rags (Luke 15:11-32)

Jesus told a story about a boy who thought obeying God was no fun. The boy asked his father for his share of money and traveled to a faraway country. He wasted all of his money on bad things. Soon he found himself without food, friends or a place to live. He ended up working on a pig farm eating the pigs' food. It didn't take long for the boy to realize that he was wrong. He went back to his father's house and begged for a job as a servant. But do you know what happened? His father gave him a big hug, some new clothes and food and welcomed him home. God is pleased when we say we are sorry. He will forgive us like the father forgave the boy who ran away.

What to Do

✴ This boy ran away from home. Follow the maze to see all of the bad places where he ended up.

How Do We Pray?

memory verse
. . . .
Humble yourselves before the Lord, and he will lift you up.   ~James 4:10

God Listens to the Humble (Luke 18:9-14)

Two men went to the temple to pray. One was a proud religious leader, called a Pharisee. The other was a tax collector who had stolen money from many people. The Pharisee stood tall and looked toward heaven and prayed, "Thank You, God, that I am not like that tax collector. I pray every day and fast and give to the poor." The tax collector was too ashamed to lift his head and prayed, "Lord, forgive me. I'm a sinner. Please have mercy on me." To which man's prayers do you think God listened?

What to Do

✱ Each man in the story prayed to God, but only one was forgiven. Follow the maze from each man to find out which one God listened to.

Climb the Tree

Zaccheus (Luke 19:1-10)

Zaccheus was a very short man. He wanted to see Jesus, but there were so many taller people watching, he couldn't see over their heads. So Zaccheus climbed up in a tree. When Jesus came by, He told Zaccheus to come down. They had lunch at Zaccheus' house. Jesus forgave Zaccheus for the wrong things he had done.

What to Do

* Follow the maze to help Zaccheus find the best branch in the tree where he can see Jesus.

Crucify Him! Crucify Him!

memory verse
. . . .
From now on, the Son of Man will be seated at the right hand of the mighty God.
~Luke 22:69

Jesus Goes to Trial (Luke 22:66-23:25)

After Jesus' arrest, He was brought before the religious leaders. These men wanted Jesus to die. They kept asking, "Are you the Son of God?" Jesus remained quiet for a long time. Finally He answered, "I am who you say I am." Many people lied about Jesus. Then Jesus was taken before the Roman ruler, Pilate. He couldn't see anything wrong with Jesus. "Jesus has done nothing wrong," Pilate told the crowd. Pilate sent Jesus to another ruler named Herod. Herod laughed at Jesus and then sent Him back to Pilate. Governor Pilate didn't want to kill Jesus. But the people yelled, "Crucify Him! Crucify Him!" Pilate was afraid that the Jews might riot. So Jesus was taken away to be killed. Jesus loved us so much that He went without an argument.

What to Do

✱ Jesus had to go before many people before finally going to the cross. Follow this maze to see where He went.

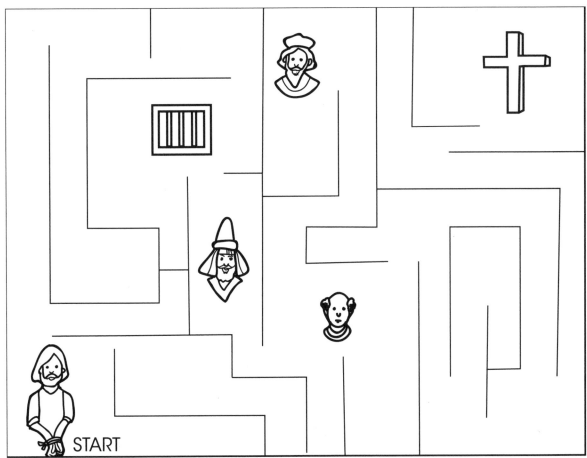

A Noble Father

memory verse
. . . .
The man took Jesus at his word. ~John 4:50

A Noble Story (John 4:43-54)

One day a royal official's son was very sick. He heard that Jesus had come into town. The man ran to Jesus and asked Him to heal his son. "Please, come and heal my son before he dies," the man begged. Jesus said, "Go. Your son will live." The man believed Jesus and went home. While on his way, his servants met him with the news that his son was healed. He asked the time when his son got better. They said, "The fever left him yesterday at the seventh hour." The father realized that was the exact time Jesus said the boy would live. The man's whole household rejoiced and believed in Jesus. Aren't you glad that Jesus is God's Son?

What to Do

✱ These pictures tell the story of the nobleman and his son, but they are all mixed up.
Can you number them in order?

A Sick Boy is Healed

memory verse
. . . .
I have shown you many great miracles.   ~John 10:32

From Sick to Saved (John 4:46-5)

A very important official of the king had a son. One day the boy became very ill and was dying. His fever got worse and worse. There was nothing his parents could do. Then the official remembered Jesus. So he traveled many miles to find Him. The father begged Jesus to come and see his son. But Jesus told him, "Go home, your son lives." The official believed Jesus. When he got home, the father found his son alive and well. Miles between them didn't keep Jesus from healing the boy. Miles between them didn't stop Jesus' love for the boy. In the same way, Jesus loves and cares for you from heaven.

What to Do

✳ Help the sad father find his way to Jesus.

A Crippled Man Walks

memory verse

Whoever hears my word and believes [in God] has eternal life. ~John 5:24

Walk! (John 5:1-15)

One day Jesus was in Jerusalem for a feast. There was a pool in Jerusalem near where the sick sat. Sometimes the waters in the pool turned hot and bubbled. The people thought it had healing powers. Jesus walked by the pool. He saw a man who had been crippled most of his life. "Do you want to walk?" Jesus asked the man. "Yes. But I have no one to lift me into the pool when it bubbles," the man replied. "Get up! Pick up your map and walk!" Jesus told the man. Suddenly the man could walk! Many people watching still didn't believe Jesus could do such things. Only God's Son can make a crippled man walk

What to Do

✳ Look at the pictures. Color the person in each row who is walking.

More than Enough to Eat

memory verse
. . . .
Give thanks to the Lord. ~Psalm 136:1

A Boy Shares His Lunch (John 6:1-15)

One day Jesus taught God's Word to thousands of people gathered on a hillside. They were so interested in what Jesus was saying that they forgot about eating. It was growing dark. The disciples told Jesus, "Send the people away so they can get something to eat." But Jesus wanted to feed them before they left. Soon they found a small boy with a basket of food. Jesus asked the little boy if he was willing to share. The boy was excited about giving his five loaves of bread and two fish to Jesus. Then Jesus thanked God for the food and passed it to the crowd. Everyone ate and ate until they were full. When they picked up the leftovers there were twelve baskets full! Do you think that little boy was happy he shared his lunch with Jesus and the crowd?

What to Do

✱ Can you count the loaves of bread and the fishes? Write the numbers in the boxes.

A Wonderful Walk

memory verse
. . . .
[Jesus said,] "It is I; don't be afraid." ~John 6:20

Walking on Water (John 6:16-21)

One day, Jesus' friends were sailing in a boat. Suddenly a storm came. The wind blew the boat. The waves grew higher and higher. The men were afraid their boat might sink. Through the rain they saw someone walking toward their boat. "It's a ghost!" they cried. "I'm not a ghost," the man replied. It was Jesus! He was walking on the water! Can you do that? Can anyone do that? God's Son can. Jesus reached the boat. As soon as He got in the storm stopped. It was very quiet. Jesus' friends were happy that He was the Son of God.

What to Do

✳ Look at the pictures. In each row, one picture is going in a different direction. Color the pictures that face the same way.

The Blind Man Sees

Jesus Gives a Man Sight (John 9:1, 6-7)

As he went along, he saw a man blind from birth . . . He spit on the ground, made some mud with the saliva, and put it on the man's eyes. "Go," he told him, "wash in the Pool of Siloam" (this word means Sent). So the man went and washed, and came home seeing.

What to Do

✳ We often take our sight for granted. But even if you need glasses, it is hard to imagine not being able to see at all. Jesus encountered a blind man who wanted to be healed. Use the Scripture for clues to fill in the crossword puzzle. The Scripture tells how Jesus healed the blind man.

Down
1. Cleansed using water
2. Being born
4. To start to move
5. Combination of sounds that have a meaning
8. Parts of the face that allow you to see
9. Human adult male
12. A small pond
13. Liquid from the mouth
14. Wet, sticky, soft earth

Across
3. To perceive with the eye
6. The solid surface of the earth
7. The place where a person resides
9. Created
10. Did come
11. Saliva
13. Directed to go
15. Unable to see
16. To cleanse using water

A Special Gift
Makes Others Angry

memory verse

Mary took...expensive perfume; she poured it on Jesus' feet and wiped his feet with her hair. ~John 12:3

A Special Gift (John 12:1-11)

Before Jesus went to Jerusalem He stopped to see His friends Lazarus, Mary and Martha, who lived in Bethany. His friends honored Jesus with a dinner. Martha served the meal, while Lazarus sat next to Jesus. But where was Mary? She was at the feet of Jesus. But this time Mary was pouring expensive perfume on His feet! She then wiped it with her hair. Judas, one of Jesus' disciples, became angry. "That was expensive! It could have been sold and the money given to the poor," he said. Judas didn't really care about the poor, though. Sometimes he would even steal from the money bag that Jesus and the disciples carried. Jesus said, "Leave her alone. She is getting me ready for my burial. You will always have the poor. But I will be gone soon." Jesus knew it was time to go to Jerusalem to die.

What to Do

* Look at the story pictures. Number the pictures in the correct order.

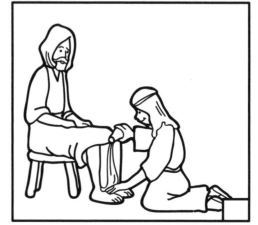

Friends of Jesus

memory verse
. . . .
You are my friends if you do what I command. ~ John 15:14

Love is Shared
Through Obedience (John 15:9-17)

Jesus talked a lot about obedience to His disciples. He said that love is shared through obedience. What does it show your parents when you obey them?

What to Do

✱ Write the first letter of each object starting with the fish to find the hidden answer in the word circle.

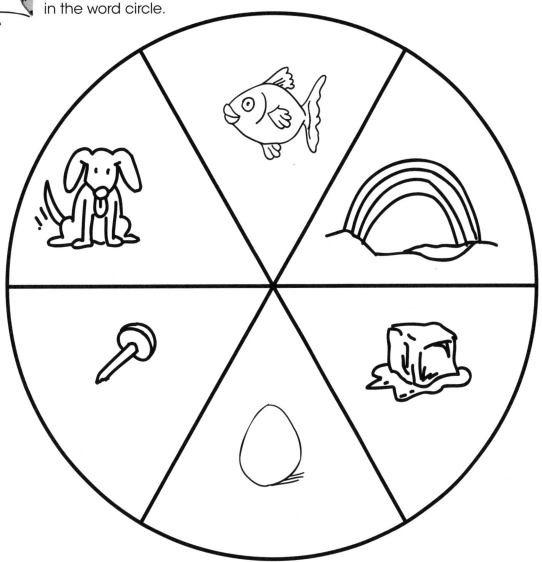

___ ___ ___ ___ ___ ___

Jesus Died for Us

A Special Gift (John 19:18-30)

Some bad men did not like that Jesus said He was the Son of God. So they nailed His hands and feet to a big wooden cross. Jesus had done nothing wrong, only good things. Jesus died on that cross. He was punished for our sins. Jesus wanted to do that. He died on a cross so that we could go to heaven with God. But the good news is that Jesus came back to life again! After three days, He came out of His tomb. He did this so that we might know that someday we too shall overcome death. We will rise and go to heaven to be with Jesus. Let's thank Jesus for dying for our sins.

What to Do

✳ Inside this gift are some sentences. They are missing words. Look at the word list. Which word would you choose to fill in the blanks? Write the words on the lines. Take the first letter of each word to fill in the blank on sentence 5.

What was Jesus' special gift to us?

1. Jesus _____ us.

2. Jesus lives _____ heaven.

3. We love Jesus because He _____ loved us.

4. Jesus loves _____.

5. Jesus gave us _____.

<u>Word List</u>
everyone
loves
in
first

Find the Hidden Fish

Jesus' Friends Go Fishing (John 21:3-14)

Peter and some of Jesus' friends went fishing. They fished and fished and fished all night, but they didn't catch any fish. Then Jesus told them where to throw their nets in the water. When they obeyed Jesus, they caught 153 fish!

What to Do

✳ Color brown all the spaces marked with a black dot. You'll find some of the fish Jesus' friends caught. How many fish did you find? You can color the rest of the picture, too

Feed My Sheep

memory verse

Take care of my sheep. ~John 21:16

Three Times (John 21:15-25)

Jesus had helped the disciples catch a net full of fish. Then they ate together. When they had finished Jesus asked Peter, "Do you love Me?" Peter answered, "Yes, Lord, You know I love You." Jesus said, "Then feed my sheep." Jesus asked again, "Peter, do you love Me?" Peter again answered, "Yes, Lord." And Jesus said, "Feed my sheep." Three times Jesus asked Peter the same question and three times He said, "Feed my sheep." This was Jesus' way of forgiving Peter for denying Him three times. We all make mistakes. Peter had made a terrible one. Do you think Peter really loved Jesus?

What to Do

✳ Jesus asked Peter, "Do you love Me?" three times. Find three sheep, three fish, three loaves of bread and three number 3s hidden in the picture.

212

The People Repent

memory verse

Repent and be baptized, every one of you, in the name of Jesus Christ for the forgiveness of your sins. ~Acts 2:38

Peter Addresses the Crowd (Acts 2:29-41)

We should repent as soon as we know we do something wrong. Jerusalem was a crowded city on the day of Pentecost. What a perfect day for the Holy Spirit to show Himself! Peter addressed the crowd and told them the story of Jesus' death and resurrection. Their immediate response was, "Brothers, what shall we do?"

What to Do

✷ What did Peter tell the crowd? Find the answer by crossing out all of the letters that have a dot in their box.

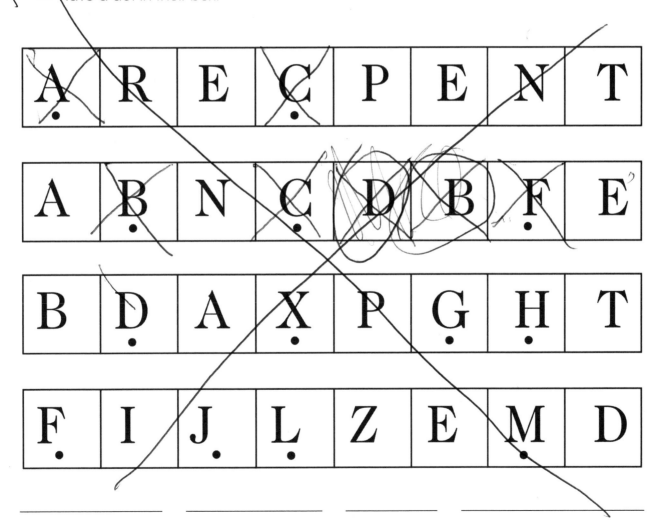

A	R	E	C	P	E	N	T

A	B	N	C	D	B	F	E

B	D	A	X	P	G	H	T

F	I	J	L	Z	E	M	D

_____

Tell the Truth Hidden Message

memory verse
....
You will know the truth, and the truth will set you free. ~John 8:32

Telling the Truth (Acts 6:12–7:53)

The men who lied about Stephen made many people angry at him! They grabbed Stephen and brought him to the temple. False witnesses said that Stephen spoke evil about God. The Jewish leaders looked at Stephen and saw that his face was like the face of an angel. They asked, "Are these charges true?" Stephen did not lie; he told the truth.

What to Do

✳ Begin the puzzle at the circled letter. Cross out the next two letters and circle the following letter. Continue crossing out two letters and circling the next letter (or number) until you come to the end of the spiral. Then go back to the first circled letter and write it in the first blank at the bottom of the page. Print the next circled letter (or number) in the next blank. Continue until all the blanks are full. Read what Stephen said to the people in the temple. Stephen told the truth, even though it made the people mad.

Stephen said,   "__ __ __

__ __ __ __ __ __ __ __

__ __ __ __ __ __ __ __ __

__ __ __ __ __ __ ... __ __ __ __

__ __ __ __ __ __ __ __ __

__ __."

__ __ __ __ __ __ __:__ __

Obeying God's Word

memory verse

I obey your word. ~Psalm 119:67

Tell Others About God (Acts 8:26-40)

One day a very important man drove his chariot from Jerusalem. He was on his way home to Ethiopia. God sent Philip to meet the man. Philip saw the man reading a scroll. The scroll was God's Word. Philip helped the man to understand the scroll. The Ethiopian obeyed God and received Jesus as his Savior. He asked to be baptized right away. Then he drove home to Ethiopia, and he was happy that he understood God's Word. God wants us to tell others about Him.

What to Do

* These pictures tell the story of the Ethiopian and Philip. But they are in the wrong order! Number them in the order that the story happened. The first one is done for you.

Philip Obeys The Angel

memory verse
....
I have promised to obey your words. ~Psalm 119:57

Go South, Philip (Acts 8:26-40)

God may have a special plan for you each day. You can't always go where you want or do what you want — but God may have someone or something special waiting for you. God sent an angel to Philip. The angel told Philip to go south. On his journey, Philip met an Ethiopian. Philip taught this man about Jesus. The man decided to follow Jesus, too.

What to Do

✳ Walk Philip through the maze. Who does he meet?

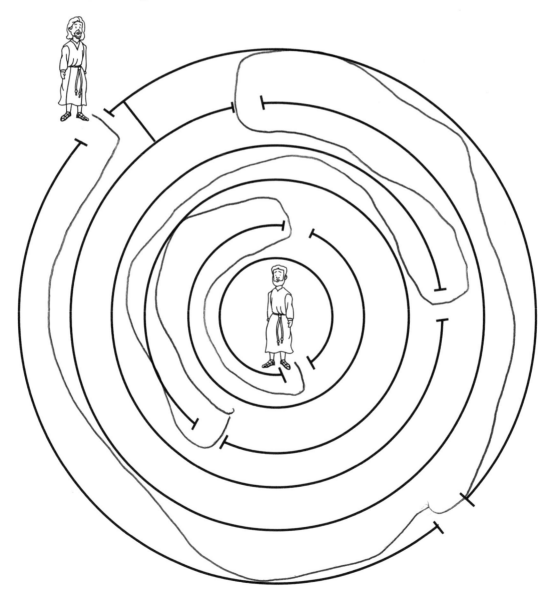

How Many Garments?

memory verse
Clothe yourselves with compassion. ~Colossians 3:12

Dorcas Helps (Acts 9:32-42)

Dorcas carefully pushed the needle into the fabric of the coat she was making, then pulled it out. The coat was for Levi, Naomi's little boy. Levi's father had died, and Naomi didn't have money for new clothes for her children. So Dorcas was happy she could help Naomi and Levi. What talent do you have that could be used to help others?

What to Do

✻ Count the clothes in each box and write the number in the square.
Then color the pictures.

Dorcas Loves Jesus

memory verse
....
Love each other as I have loved you. ~John 15:12

Love Others (Acts 9:36-42)

Dorcas was always helping others. She listened when they were sad. She fed them when they had no food. She helped them when they were sick. Dorcas' favorite thing to do was to make clothes for people. Dorcas knew that to love and obey Jesus, she must love others and take care of them.

What to Do

✱ In each row, color the pictures that belong together.

A Joyful Servant

memory verse
. . . .
His servants will serve him. ~Revelations 22:3

An Angel Frees Peter (Acts 12:1-17)

King Herod wanted to get rid of the Christians. Peter and James were in prison for teaching about Jesus. Herod killed James and planned to kill Peter, too. The Christians were at Mary's house praying. God sent an angel to free Peter from prison in answer to their prayers. Peter went to Mary's house. A servant girl named Rhoda came to the door. She ran to tell the others that Peter was there. She was so excited she forgot to let him in! The other Christians didn't believe her. But she insisted. Peter kept knocking. Finally they opened the door. They were all happy that Peter was alive. Rhoda had told the truth.

What to Do

✳ Rhoda was so excited, she forgot to OPEN the door. Color the doors below that are OPEN.

219

Places to Tell About Jesus

Paul Tells About Jesus (Acts 13–23)

Paul traveled all around telling people about Jesus. Sometimes people were happy to hear about Jesus. Other times, what Paul said about Jesus made people mad. Paul did not let anything stop him from telling people that Jesus would forgive their sins.

Paul was one of the first missionaries. Missionaries are people who often go far away to tell others about Jesus.

Paul told many people all over his world about Jesus. You can tell people in your neighborhood about Jesus, too.

What to Do

* Follow the trail to help Katie find her way to her school, her church, the playground, a friend's house and the grocery store. You can tell people about Jesus at all those places

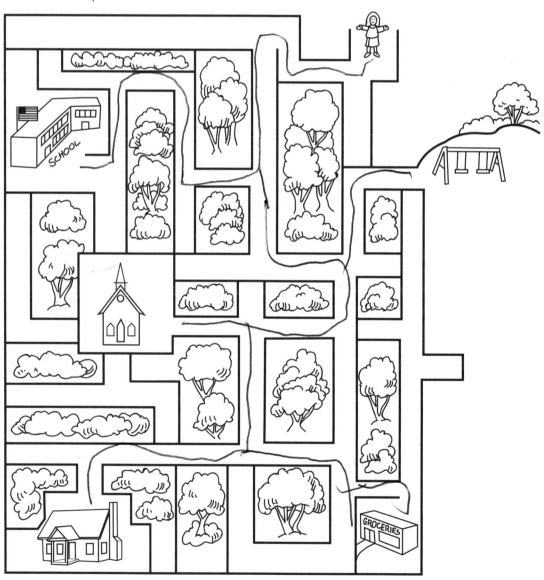

Singing Songs of Praise

memory verse

Sing for joy to God our strength. ~Psalm 81:1

Two Special Men (Acts 16:16-40)

The New Testament tells a story of two special men named Paul and Silas. These men told people about Jesus. Some people hated them for speaking about Jesus. Bad men put Paul and Silas in jail. Do you think Paul and Silas forgot about God in jail? No, they began to sing praises to God. Do you think you would sing songs if you were in jail? They loved God very much, didn't they?

What to Do

✳ Look carefully! There are five differences between these two pictures. Can you name them?

Praises in Prison

 memory verse
· ·
I will praise the Lord. ~Psalm 146:2

Paul and Silas (Acts 16:22-40)

Paul continued to tell people about Jesus. Many people hated Paul. One day some bad men put Paul and his friend Silas in jail. But Paul and Silas trusted God. They never stopped obeying Him. While in prison Paul and Silas sang about Jesus. God loves to hear our songs of praise.

 ## What to Do

✱ There are 5 things wrong in this picture. Can you find them? Circle them, then color the picture.

A Brave Young Boy

memory verse
. . . .
I will protect their lives. ~Jeremiah 49:11

A Smart Boy (Acts 23:12-22)

The Apostle Paul was in prison. While he was there his nephew heard a big crowd of men talking about a secret plan. He pretended not to hear, but he listened to every word. Forty men planned to kill Paul. The men promised not to eat anything until they had done this terrible deed. Paul's nephew ran to the prison and told his uncle the plan. He called the guard and asked him to listen to his nephew's story. The guard did not want Paul killed so he had extra soldiers sneak Paul out in the night. Paul escaped because his nephew loved him and was not afraid.

What to Do

✳ Paul's nephew did not let anyone see him listening. Can you find him?

Paul's Nephew

Worshipping God with Our Mouths

memory verse
....
Tell of his works with songs of joy. ~Psalm 107:22

Paul Speaks to a King (Acts 25:13-26:32)

One special way of worshipping God is by telling others about Jesus. Paul loved to tell people about God's Son. Paul was arrested for talking about Jesus. One day King Agrippa wanted to talk to Paul. He wanted to see what Paul had to say. What do you think Paul talked about? Jesus, of course! Paul was not afraid to tell the king about his Savior. He wanted King Agrippa to worship Jesus, too. King Agrippa came very close to believing in Jesus. But not close enough. Who could you tell about Jesus?

What to Do

* These pictures tell the story but they are all mixed up. Can you number them in the correct order? The first one is done for you.

Paul is Shipwrecked

memory verse

I have faith in God. ~Acts 27:25

Safe on the Shore (Acts 27)

The New Testament tells a story of a brave man named Paul. Paul had to go to Rome. The king in Rome was going to decide if Paul should die. Paul was taken to Rome on a ship. A storm came and the ship was in trouble. The storm blew big waves over the ship. But Paul wasn't afraid. He trusted God. The other people were afraid. They didn't believe in God and thought the ship would sink. God told Paul that He would take care of him. God said that the ship would crash, but no one would die. Paul told the others what God said. Soon they saw some land. The ship crashed on the land. Paul and the others swam to the shore. Everyone was safe. God had a special plan for Paul. God has a special plan for you, too.

What to Do

✳ **Paul's ship is wrecked.** Can you help him swim to the shore?

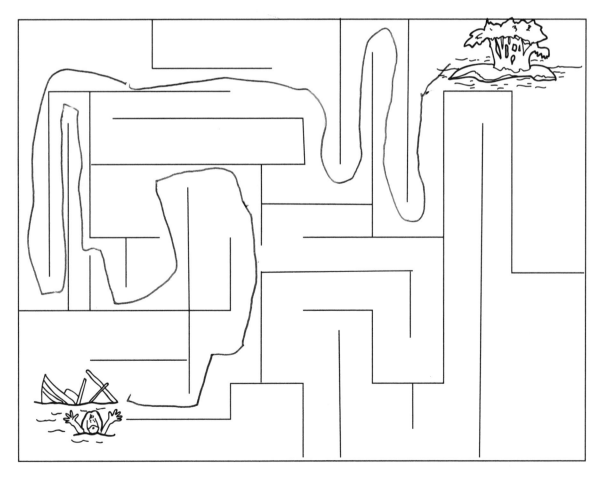

Good News Crossword Puzzle

memory verse
Whoever believes in the Son has eternal life. ~John 3:36

Dying and Rising Again (1 Corinthians 15:1-8; 1 Timothy 1:15)

Why did the Son of God become a human? Was it to teach us about God? Was it to heal the sick? He did those things and much more. But the real reason He came was to die. As a human, He could die for our sins. Because He is God, He rose again. He came to save sinners and take them to heaven one day, if they believe in Him.

What to Do

✱ Look up the verses below, find the missing word in each sentence, and print it in the puzzle. Then unscramble the circled letters to discover what the Good News of salvation is called.

Across

1. All have sinned and come short of the _____ of God. (Romans 3:23) KJV

3. We believe that Jesus died and _____ again. (1 Thessalonians 4:14) KJV

4. Whosoever believeth in him should not _____. (John 3:16) KJV

5. I give unto them _____ life. (John 10:28) KJV

Down

2. _____ died for our sins. (1 Corinthians 15:3) KJV

3. _____ and turn to God. (Acts 26:20)

6. I am come that they might have _____. (John 10:10) KJV

What is the Good News of salvation called?

The _____

226

Setting a Good Example

memory verse

Don't let anyone look down on you because you are young. ~1 Timothy 4:12

Learning from Letters (1 Timothy 4:11-16)

Timothy and the Apostle Paul were good friends. Timothy liked listening to Paul tell stories about Jesus. Paul took Timothy with him to teach God's Word. Timothy grew to be a strong leader in the church even though he was young. When Paul was not with Timothy he wrote the boy letters. These letters became part of the New Testament. We can learn from these letters to Timothy. In them, Paul tells Timothy to set a good example for others to follow. That is a good lesson for us, too.

What to Do

* Timothy was a good example. We can set good examples, too. Draw a line from Timothy on the left column to a person who is following his example in the column on the right.

BEE-ing Fair

memory verse

Do what is right and just.   ~Proverbs 21:3

Paul Writes a Letter (1 Timothy 5; 2 Timothy 1:5–6)

One day Paul wrote Timothy a letter. "Dear Timothy," the letter began, "don't forget the teaching and stories your mother and grandmother taught you. Be fair. Don't show favor." Paul was Timothy's hero. Timothy knew that Paul taught only the truth. Timothy asked God to help him to be fair and to follow all of Paul's instructions to do only what was right and fair.

What to Do

✳ A bee is fair when it leaves some nectar for another bee. We can be fair when we take one cookie and leave the other for a friend. God wants us to be fair.

Color all the spaces with the word "fair" blue, and the spaces with the word "bee" yellow.

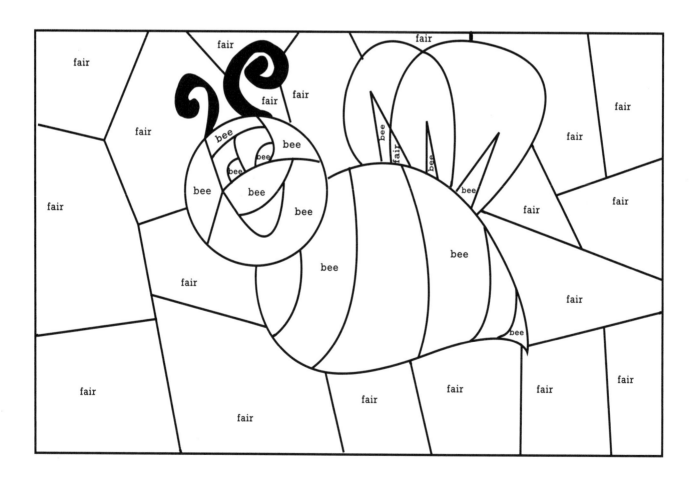

A Boy Becomes a Missionary

memory verse

He said to them, "Go into all the world and preach the good news to all creation."

~Mark 16:15

Spread God's Word (2 Timothy 1:5; Acts 16:1-5)

Timothy loved God. He loved God because his mother and his grandmother loved God. They told him all about God. They prayed with him every day. They read God's Word to him, too. One day Paul came to their town. He told Timothy and his family about Jesus. They were happy to learn about God's Son. Paul asked Timothy to go with him to tell others about Jesus. Timothy was happy to join Paul on his missionary journeys. You can be a missionary too. You don't have to go to far away lands. Whom do you know who you could tell about Jesus?

What to Do

✳ These children want to tell others about God. Their teacher has a box with 12 Bibles. She is going to give each child Bibles to give to other people. Each child should get the same number of Bibles. Write the number of Bibles each child will get on the line nearest to him or her.

Listening to Your Parents

memory verse

Do not forsake your mother's teaching. ~Proverbs 1:8

Timothy Learns (2 Timothy 1:5)

The Bible tells about a boy who loved listening to God's Word. His name was Timothy. His mother's name was Eunice and his grandmother's name was Lois. They loved God and His Word, too. They taught Timothy the laws written in God's Word. They told him stories about Abraham, Moses and David. They taught Timothy to work hard and to be obedient. Timothy listened very carefully to his mother and grandmother. He obeyed them and God's Law. Timothy grew into a young man who loved God very much.

What to Do

✽ Can you find five things in the top picture that are different from the bottom picture? Can you find eleven?

The **SUPER-SIZED BOOK**
Of BIBLE PUZZLES

ANSWERS

Answer Pages

Page 13
Let's Hide Word Search

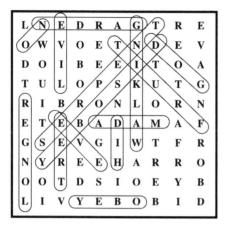

Page 14
When Temptation Strikes

Submit yourselves, then, to God. Resist the devil, and he will flee from you.   James 4:7

Page 15
God Delivers a Baby

First on top left matches third on bottom; second on top matches last on bottom; third on top matches first on bottom; last on top matches second on bottom.

Page 16
Follow the Motions

Page 17
The First Family

Shepherd's staff is above water; spear is vertical at bottom left; hoe is vertical between woman and shepherd; needle and thread are at top right near leaves.

Page 18
Noah's Sons Work Hard

Bucket matches hose; oil lamp matches electric lamp; manger matches bed; basket of fruit matches shopping cart; thread spool matches sewing machine.

Page 19
Is Dad Crazy?

Dots form an ark

Page 20
How to Float a Zoo

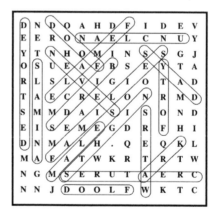

Hidden message: Noah did everything just as God commanded him.

Answer Pages

Page 22
Animal Hunt

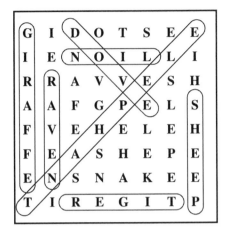

Page 23
Dry Land Code

THE DOVE FOUND DRY LAND

Page 24
The Long Voyage

It rained for forty days and forty nights. Noah first sent out a raven and then a dove to find dry land. The dove found an olive leaf.

Page 25
The Dove Returns to the Ark

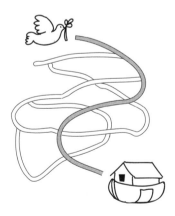

Page 26
Mystery Word

rainbow

Page 27
The Big Tower

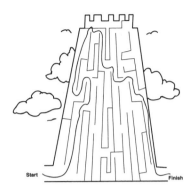

Page 28
Abraham Moves to Canaan

CANAAN

Page 30
A Special Son

Row 1: bottle; row 2: safety pin; row 3: teddy bear.

Page 31
A Faithful Father

FAITH

Page 32
God Cares for Abraham's Son

Finish drawing bush; dots form angel; water came from rocks.

Page 33
Sarah Has a Son

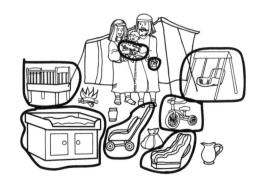

Answer Pages

Page 34
Isaac Is Born

Page 35
Find the Sheep

Page 37
Twin Brothers

Differences in bottom picture: Esau is missing arrows and belt buckle and is wearing pants; Jacob is missing his headband and is wearing a necklace; the sheep has glasses.

Page 38
Very Different Twins

Esau: knife, bow, arrows, deer, outdoor bed; Jacob: pot, sheep, tents, hoe

Page 39
Happy Are the Peacemakers

Page 40
WHO? Worksheet

1. Isaac, 2. Rebekah, 3. Esau, 4. Jacob

Page 41
Honest Before God

DECEIT

Page 42
A Father of Many Sons

Page 43
Tricked into Marriage

Rachel and Leah

Page 44
Stained Glass Forgiveness

FORGIVE

Answer Pages

Page 45
An Obedient Son

Row 1: third sheep missing ear; row 2: second basket missing handle; row 3: fourth sheave missing top; row 4: third jar missing handles.

Page 47
His Only Possession Puzzle

His faith in God

Page 48
Circle the Picture

house, jail, dry well

Page 49
A Story to Tell

Clockwise from top left: 1, 4, 2, 3

Page 50
Forgiveness Word Search

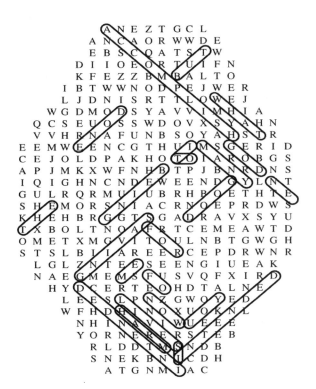

Page 51
A Princess Rescues a Baby

Page 52
Helping the Family

Circle: broom and dust pan; fed dog; dish and cloth; baby and bottle.

Page 53
Who Sees Me Puzzle

GOD

Page 54
Moses Stands Up to Pharaoh

Clockwise from top left: 3, 4, 1, 2.

Page 55
Plague Word Search

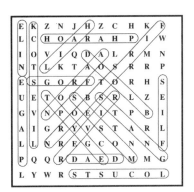

Answer Pages

Page 56
Ten Warnings

Three frogs; six locusts; eight flies.

Page 57
Moses Crosses the Red Sea

Page 58
Heading for the Promised Land

Top picture's dots form a cloud; draw fire in bottom picture.

Page 59
Match the Facts

1. C
2. E
3. F
4. G
5. D
6. A
7. H
8. B

Page 60
Crossing the Red Sea

Bottom left chariot is different.

Page 61
Ten Rules to Obey

Dots form the Ten Commandment tablets.

Page 62
Rules About God

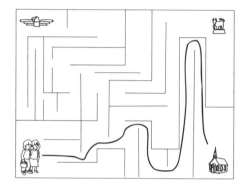

Page 63
The Ten Commandments

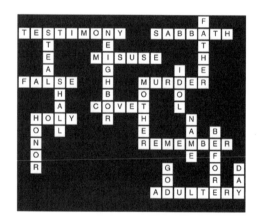

Page 64
The Golden Calf

Answer Pages

Page 65
The Israelites Are Sorry

7 snakes

Page 66
God Tells His People to Obey Him

"Obey Your Mother and Father" matches boy helping man; "Make God's Day Special" matches people going to church; "Do Not Steal" matches child taking candy.

Page 67
God Gives His People Rules

HEART

Page 68
Obey and Don't Be Afraid

squares = five

circles = six

triangles = eight

Page 69
God is Always There Maze

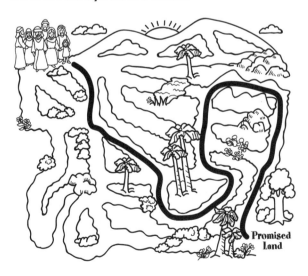

Page 70
Joshua Fights a Battle

Page 71
Jericho Falls

Row 1: different one is last; row 2: different one is second; row 3: different one is third; row 4: different one is second.

Page 72
God's Rules Are Good

broom, dish, doll, Bible

Page 73
Hidden Message Puzzle

Page 74
Gideon Defeats His Enemies

Jars are 1 second row, 1 third row, 1 fourth row; swords are 1 first row, 2 second row, 1 third row, 2 fourth row; torches are 3 first row, 3 second row, 1 third row, 3 fourth row.

Answer Pages

Page 75
A Boy of Great Strength

Mane and hair.

Page 76
A Boy Shows Kindness

Page 77
A Faithful Friend

In bottom picture: Ruth has no vest, a tied belt and no shoes; Naomi has no hair bangs, no ear, no headband, no belt and no shoes.

Page 78
A Daughter-in-Law's Devotion

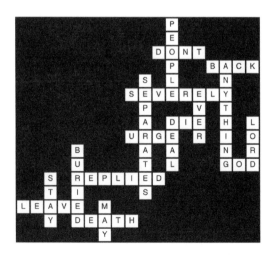

Page 79
Gleaning Code

To glean means you share because you care.

Page 80
A Mother Keeps Her Promise

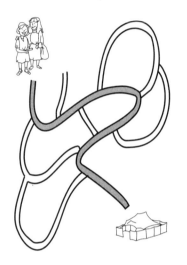

Page 81
Easy or Hard

For no matter how many promises God has made, they are "Yes" in Christ. (2 Corinthians 1:20)

Page 82
Joyful Letters

GOD GIVES ME JOY

Page 83
Disobedient Sons

Top left column and second right column; second left column and bottom right column; third left column and third right column; bottom left column and top right column

Page 84
Eli's Wicked Sons

Row 1: left; row 2: middle; row 3: right

Answer Pages

Page 85
Samuel Obeys God's Call

Lamb is at head of bed; oil lamp is in pillow; water pitcher is near foot of bed; scroll is in fold of sheet; patched robe is at foot of bed.

Page 86
Finding God's Word

BIBLE

Page 87
Interference in My Life

Page 88
Samuel Finds Israel a King

There are 11 crowns in the picture.

Page 89
Find the Donkeys

Page 90
God Chooses David

13

Page 91
David Serves Saul

Dove, glove

Page 92
A Shepherd Boy

Lions: in right side of tree and in bushes; bears: in clouds and in left side of tree

Page 93
Help with Fighting Giants

1. David
2. Goliath
3. Saul
4. slingshot
5. Bethlehem
Go and the Lord be with you.

Page 94
Obedience Kills a Giant

In bottom picture: soldier behind David; David wearing helmet; David carrying bow, arrows and sword; Goliath missing helmet; Goliath missing sword; Goliath wearing tied vest, Goliath is shorter

Page 95
Good Friends

THEY DO WHAT A FRIEND ASKS

Page 96
David Shows Mercy

M	E	R	C	Y
O	G	I	A	O
O	G	N	T	Y
N		G		O

Answer Pages

Page 97
Kindness to a Crippled Boy

N and S on Mephibosheth's shirt; I on his leg; S, N and K on David's robe; D and E on his throne.

Page 99
Kind King David

Page 100
Friends Forever

Crown is on Mephibosheth's arm; spoon is in his hair; book is on his tunic; crutch is on David's robe; oil lamp is on his arm.

Page 101
Training a King

God

Page 102
Where Can I Worship God?

CAR

CHURCH

HOME

BEDROOM

SCHOOL

Page 103
A Wise King

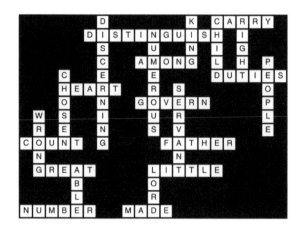

Page 104
Building God's House

Page 105
Bad Friends

Top picture: Idol; bottom picture; friends

Page 106
God Takes Care of Elijah

The black and yellow colors reveal a raven.

Answer Pages

Page 107
Ravens Feed Elijah

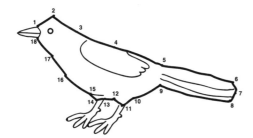

Page 109
Elisha Follows Elijah

In bottom picture: Elijah is not pointing and has no mustache; Elisha has no headband; three stones are missing from the path; a cloud is missing from behind Elijah's head; a stone is missing from the field.

Page 110
The Prophet's Quiz

Elijah

Page 111
Learning a Lesson in Respect

Top on left matches middle on right; middle on left matches bottom on right; bottom on left matches top on right.

Page 112
A Widow Keeps Her Sons

11

Page 113
Hospitality for a Prophet

Lines should be drawn from the boy to all illustrations

Page 114
Helping Her Master

Three 7s are in the left, middle and right sides of the grass; one 7 is on Naaman's hand; one 7 is on his tunic; one 7 is in his hair; the last 7 is in the right center of the water.

Page 115
Obeying the Law of God

Dots form a Bible

Page 116
King Josiah Finds God's Word

Your Word is a lamp to my feet and a light to my path.

Page 117
Thanking God

THANKS

Page 118
Worshipping in God's House

Lamp, cowboy hat, phone, popcorn and soda

Page 119
Hezekiah Repents of His Pride

PRIDE

Page 120
Repairing the Walls

The top left stone fits the bottom right space; the bottom left stone fits the top right space; the top right stone fits the bottom left space; and the bottom right stone fits the top left space

Answer Pages

Page 121
Nehemiah Looks at the Walls of Jerusalem

The horse is in the right side of the wall, facing the left.

Page 122
The Secret of Strength Hidden Message

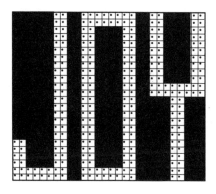

Page 123
Esther Saves Her People

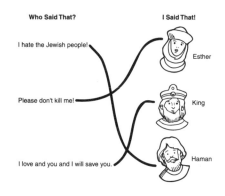

Page 124
Outside-Inside Plans

1. false

2. true

3. false

4. true

5. false

6. false

7. false

8. true

9. true

10. true

11. false

BEAUTY, HEART

Page 125
A Beautiful Queen Obeys

Lines should be drawn from Esther to the long dress, fancy shoes, necklace and crown.

Page 126
Esther Obeys Mordecai's Instruction

Esther is at top left.

Page 127
Hearing the Truth Maze

Answer Pages

Page 128
A Dangerous Decree

An order usually having the force of the law.

Page 129
Job Obeys No Matter What

Clockwise from top left: 1, 3, 2, 4

Page 130
Job's Friends Try to Make Him Disobey

Page 132
God Uses Children

DAVID; JOASH; SAMUEL; MOSES; JOSIAH

Page 133
God Made Me for a Special Purpose

I AM ONLY A CHILD

Page 134
The King's Food

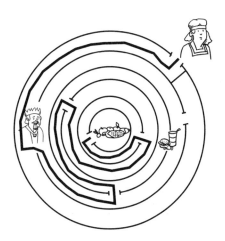

Page 135
Far From Home

Cross should be circled; all others crossed out

Page 136
Who's the King?

duck   elephant

lion   zebra

skunk   egg

King Belshazzar

Page 137
Daniel in the Lions' Den

Lion at bottom has upward tail.

Answer Pages

Page 138
A Den Full of Lions

Page 139
Disobedience Smells Fishy

Dots form a big fish.

Page 140
A Big Fish

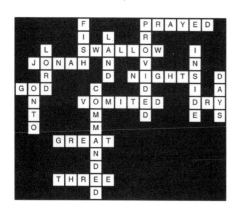

Page 141
Back on the Road to Nineveh

Page 142
Teaching Others to Obey

Jonah is in the center.

Page 144
Mary and Joseph Obey the Angel

Row 1: second angel missing feet; row 2: second man missing bag on roll and camel missing one back leg; row 3: manger missing back right slat; row 4: second picture missing sun

Page 145
Warning Code

Flee to Egypt.

Page 146
The Long Journey Maze

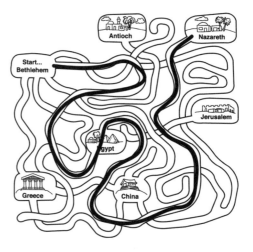

Answer Pages

Page 147
A Secret Message

jar	open	hat
nest	baby	apple
pan	top	ice
zoo	east	down
Jesus	easy	ship
under	see	

Final answer: John baptized Jesus.

Page 148
New Life Puzzle

John the Baptist

Page 149
Run From Satan

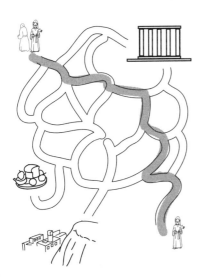

Page 150
Fisherman of Men

19 fish; men

Page 151
The Beatitudes

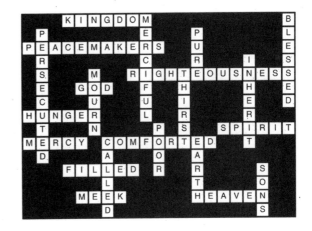

Page 153
Let Your Light Shine

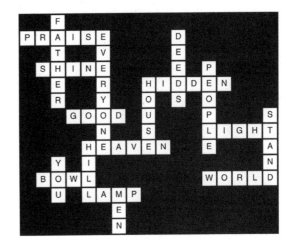

Answer Pages

Page 154
Where Do We Pray?

Page 155
Be Clean!

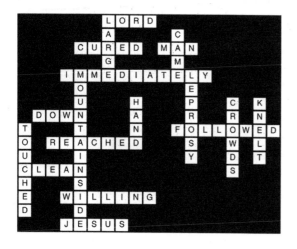

Page 156
Matthew Obeys Jesus

Tree is upside-down; car on street; man is wearing polka dots; bull is eating money

Page 157
Jairus' Daughter Brought to Life

Clockwise from top left: 1, 2, 3, 4.

Page 158
Nothing Is Impossible

Row 1: boy on left; row 2: seed on right; row 3: mouse on left.

Page 159
Blessed Are the Merciful

Clockwise from top left: 3, 4, 2, 1.

Page 160
Let the Little Children Come

Second from top on left matches fourth from top on right; fourth from top on left matches second from top on right.

Page 161
A Story About Two Sons

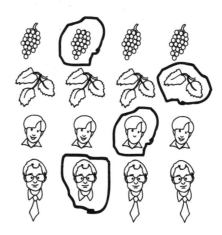

Page 162
A Friend Shares His Tomb

Clockwise from top left: 2, 3, 4, 1, 5.

Answer Pages

Page 163
The First Easter

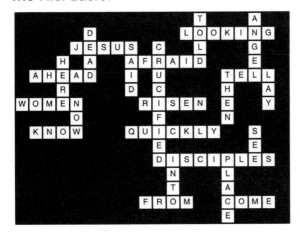

Page 164
A Man Comes Through the Roof

Missing in second one: people peeking over edge, man at far left's feet, rope holding cot on right side.

Page 165
Jesus Prepares a Big Lunch

Page 166
Find the Hidden Pictures

Page 167
A Rich Young Man

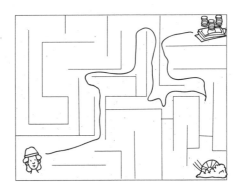

Page 168
The Fig Tree

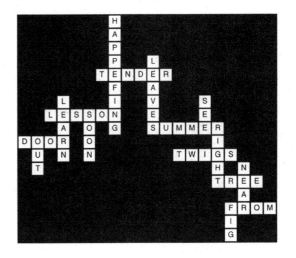

Page 169
An Empty Tomb

stone

afraid

alive

Page 170
Special Cousins

Top on left matches bottom on right; middle on left matches top on right; bottom on left matches middle on right.

Answer Pages

Page 171
Let Your Fingers Do the Talking

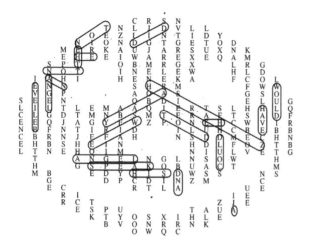

Page 172
Prepare the Way

JOHN

Page 173
Special News Telegram

Mary is the mother to the Son of God.

Page 174
An Angel Tells Good News

Page 175
A Trip to Bethlehem

Missing in second illustration: donkey, left sheep's face, Mary's face, right sheep's legs, stripes on manger, middle sheep's right ear.

Page 176
The Birth of God's Son

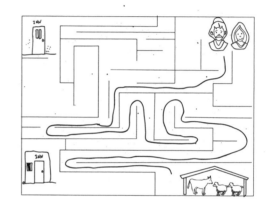

Page 177
A Child Is Born!

(7) light bulb above; giraffe; donkey has sheep's body; cow has cylinders rather than horns and shoes on its feet; donkey at right has glasses; shepherd is holding a pitchfork

Page 178
Good News!

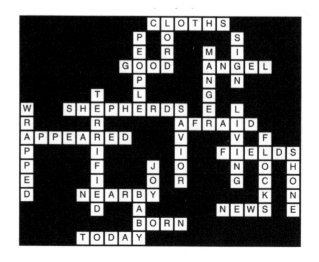

Answer Pages

Page 179
Angels Tell Shepherds the Good News

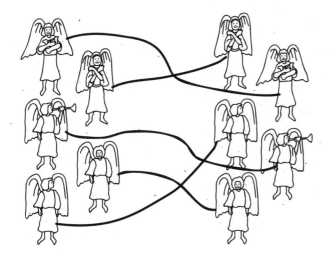

Page 183
In My Father's House

Page 180
Giving Him to God

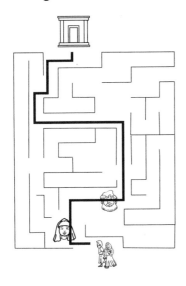

Page 185
Always Obedient

Row 1: horse; row 2: tree; row 3: boat scene

Page 181
Dot-toDot Jesus

GOD

Page 186
The New Testament

Page 182
Where to Find Jesus

BIBLE

Answer Pages

Page 187
A High Fever

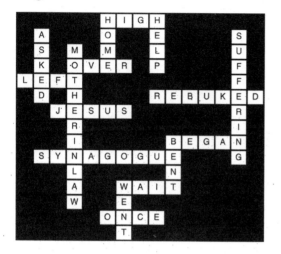

Page 188
Help the Friends Find Jesus

Page 189
A Wise Builder

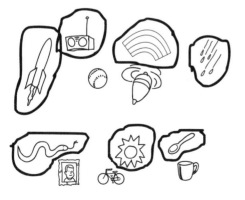

Page 190
A Boy Lives Again

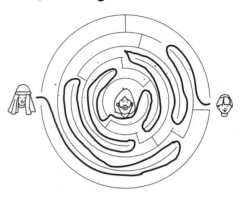

Page 191
A Wild Man Is Healed

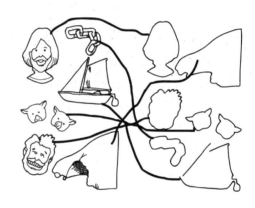

Page 192
Jesus Wipes Away Our Tears

Top face: sad; bottom face: happy.

Answer Pages

Page 193
Crippled

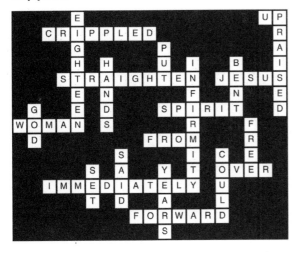

Page 194
The Mustard Seed

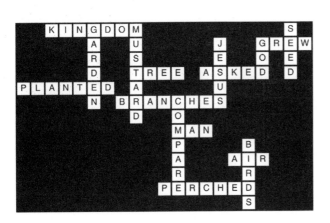

Page 195
A Good Shepherd

Page 196
A Lost Coin

Page 197
Party Time Word Search

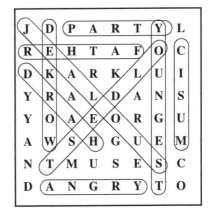

Page 198
The Boy Who Ran Away

Answer Pages

Page 199
How Do We Pray?

Page 200
Climb the Tree

Page 201
Crucify Him! Crucify Him!

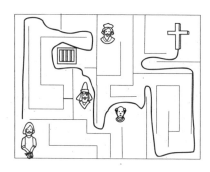

Page 202
A Noble Father

Clockwise from top left: 1, 3, 2, 4.

Page 203
A Sick Boy Is Healed

Page 205
More than Enough to Eat

Two fish; five loaves.

Page 206
A Wonderful Walk

Going the same way:

Row 1: 1, 2 & 3

Row 2: 1, 2 & 3

Row 3: 1, 2 & 4

Row 4: 1, 2 & 4

Row 5: 1, 3 & 4

Page 207
The Blind Man Sees

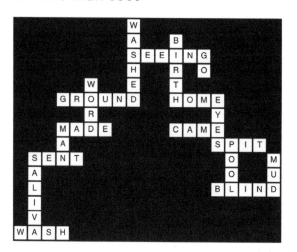

Answer Pages

Page 208
A Special Gift Makes Others Angry

Clockwise from top left: 3, 1, 2, 4.

Page 209
Friends of Jesus

FRIEND

Page 210
Jesus Died for Us

1. Jesus loves us.

2. Jesus lives in heaven.

3. We love Jesus because He first loved us.

4. Jesus loves everyone.

5. Jesus gave us life.

Page 211
Find the Hidden Fish

4 fish

Page 212
Feed My Sheep

Page 213
The People Repent

REPENT AND BE BAPTIZED

Page 214
Tell the Truth Hidden Message

Stephen said, "You who have received the law… have not obeyed it." – Acts 7:53

Page 215
Obeying God's Word

Clockwise from top right: 1, 4, 2, 3

Page 216
Philip Obeys the Angel

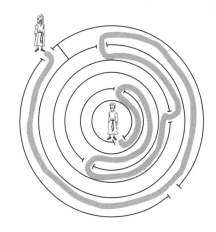

Page 217
How Many Garments?

Top row, from left 2, 5, 3;
bottom row, from left: 4, 6, 1.

Page 218
Dorcas Loves Jesus

Cloth, tape, thread; shoes, jacket, robe; bread, meat, apple; glass, bowl, plate.

Page 219
A Joyful Servant

Left and right doors are open; middle door is closed.

Answer Pages

Page 220
Places to Tell About Jesus

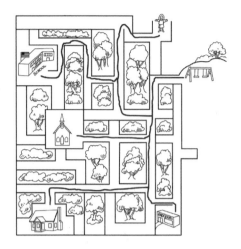

Page 221
Singing Songs of Praise

Different in second picture: bars not on window, stripes not on left man's sleeves, right man missing beard, right man has rope instead of shackles on left foot, floor is clean.

Page 222
Praises in Prison

What is wrong: balloons; mouse with cat tail; mittens on right man; right man's stool missing leg; left man missing shoe.

Page 223
A Brave Young Boy

Paul's nephew is in the middle top, just right of center.

Page 224
Worshipping God with Our Mouths

Clockwise from 1: 2, 3, 4

Page 225
Paul is Shipwrecked

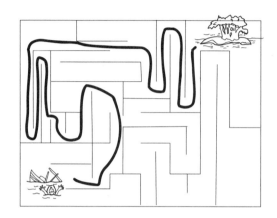

Page 226
Good News Crossword Puzzle
Secret word: GOSPEL

Page 227
Setting a Good Example

Top on left matches middle on right; middle on left matches bottom on right; bottom on left matches top on right.

Answer Pages

Page 229
A Boy Becomes a Missionary

4, 4, 4

Page 230
Listening To Your Parents

In bottom picture: boy is wearing ball cap, tie and watch; Lois is wearing cowboy hat, glasses and no fringe on belt; Eunice is wearing collar, belt with no strings and carrying purse; fish is floating on ground; ground lines are missing.

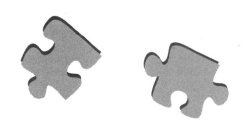